1

ISBN:979-8-9990779-0-5

This book is intended as a practical resource and
informational guide. It is not a substitute for professional
counseling or therapy. The author and publisher assume
no liability for outcomes related to the use of this book.

YOU CAN'T OPTIMIZE THIS

Why Your Success Tactics
Don't Work in Your Relationship

by

Ethan Starke

The Traffic Jam No One Talks About

You're smart. You've built something. Maybe a company, a brand, a reputation. Maybe all three.
 You know how to run a team, close a deal, and scale a vision.
 And yet — when it comes to love, intimacy, and real connection — you feel stuck.
 Worse, you're not even sure what's broken.

This book is about that hidden traffic jam.
 Not the one on the freeway — the one inside you.
 The one between who you are in the world and how you show up at home.
 The one between your sharp, optimized mind… and your half-lit, fumbling heart.

You're not alone.

In conference rooms and coffee shops across the country, a generation of high performers is quietly unraveling where it matters most — not in business, but in relationship. Behind the sharp suits and smart watches are frayed conversations, silences that scream, and relationships dying of malnourishment.

What Happened to Us?

Rewind a century or two, and intimacy was simple, if not always easy. People built lives side by side — not curated, not optimized, but *shared*. Conversations happened without checking your phone. Disagreements ended in eye contact, not ghosting. Love was messy, but it was *present*.

5

Somewhere along the way, we swapped presence for performance.

We engineered ourselves for efficiency, success, and optimization.
 We became masters of leverage and strategy — in business, in branding, even in dating.
 We gamified connection, streamlined emotion, outsourced vulnerability.

It worked — for a while. We made money. Built audiences. Dominated markets.

But something didn't scale: **intimacy.**

The Cost of High Performance

We live in a culture where success is visible and relationships are invisible.
 Where we brag about morning routines, but can't admit we haven't touched our partner in weeks.
 Where we read 10 books on negotiation but none on conflict resolution in love.

There is a human traffic jam happening in the lives of ambitious people:

- They know how to hire, but not how to *hear.*

- They can deliver a keynote, but stumble in a heartfelt apology.

- They have vision for everything — except how to be truly known.

This isn't a crisis of romance. It's a crisis of relational literacy.
And it's affecting not just individuals, but our culture — how we date, marry, parent, and live.

The Awakening We Need

If this book does anything, let it name the quiet thing you've felt but couldn't articulate:
That the mindset that built your success is sabotaging your relationships.

You can't schedule emotional connection.
You can't delegate trust.
You can't automate presence.

It's time to awaken. Not just as individuals, but as a generation.

We need to unlearn the illusion that performance equals value.
We need to remember that love is not something you earn — it's something you *allow*.
And we need to rebuild our relationships with the same courage we used to build our businesses.

This book won't flatter you.
But it will *free* you.

Welcome to the shift.

The Optimization Trap

The Ritual and the Void

He wakes at 4:45 a.m.
 Cardio. Cold plunge. Journaling. Maca root smoothie. No phone until 6:30.

His life is a system. Every minute accounted for, every ritual measured for ROI.
 By 8 a.m., he's three wins into the day.
 By 9, he's locked into a call with a venture partner.
 By 10, he's already mentally repackaging a failed product into a new vertical.

He's a builder. A machine. A force of discipline and insight.

At 10:03, his phone buzzes. It's a message from his partner:
 "Can we talk tonight?"

His stomach tightens — not because he's done something wrong,
 but because he already knows what's coming: another conversation he can't optimize.

You've been here.
 Not in that exact house. Not with that exact message.
 But in that moment — when someone you love needs more of you, and you have nothing left but tactics.

You freeze. Or offer advice. Or pivot to logistics:
 "Let's schedule a time."
 "Can we do this after your work trip?"
 "I just need a little clarity on what you need from me."

You're not dodging.
You're not cruel.
You're just wired to solve.

This is the Optimization Trap.

You've learned to lead with logic.
To control outcomes. To dominate time.
You've trained your nervous system to treat uncertainty as a threat.
And in business, it works.
In strategy, it wins.
In relationships, it quietly kills everything that matters.

This trap doesn't come with flashing lights or dramatic explosions.
It looks like routines that get tighter while your conversations get shorter.
It looks like performance reviews disguised as date nights.
It looks like a partner who can't quite explain what's wrong — only that they feel more alone the more "present" you are.

Here's the truth:
You didn't fall behind emotionally. You outpaced your humanity.

You optimized your life so well
 that the parts of you that don't scale — presence, softness, emotional nuance —
 got left behind.

You didn't mean to.
 But you treated love like a workflow:

- Connection became a scheduled task.

- Conflict became a misalignment.

- Vulnerability became a liability.

- Intimacy became inefficient.

And without knowing it,
 you started living with your partner the way you live inside a spreadsheet:
 organized, impressive, and completely disconnected from the texture of being human.

That tightening in your chest when they say, *"We need to talk"*?
 That's not dread. That's exposure.

Because you know how to solve a $3 million problem in 20 minutes —
 but you don't know what to do when someone looks at you and says:
 "I just need you to be here with me."

This chapter isn't going to tell you how to fix that.
 Because that's the whole point.
 You don't fix it.

You don't "figure it out."
 You don't optimize it.

You confront the void you built around yourself —
 the one that protects you from feeling messy, needed, vulnerable, and real.

That's the first step.
Not presence.
Not empathy.
Not love.

Awareness.

The awareness that your most finely tuned habits
have become walls your partner can't feel through.

And until you see that,
you'll keep improving —
and they'll keep disappearing.

The Success Mindset That Silences Love

Let's start with something uncomfortable:
You believe you're good at relationships.

Not in the rom-com, hand-written-poems, Nicholas Sparks
kind of way.
But in the *I-show-up / I-don't-cheat / I-handle-my-shit* kind
of way.
You don't disappear.
You don't raise your voice.
You don't play games.

In your mind, that makes you a good partner.

And here's the catch:
You're not wrong — by *your* standards.
But that's the problem.

Your standards were built for performance, not connection.

You've been conditioned to treat your life as a system.
And systems reward clarity, structure, effort, and measurable outcomes.

So, unconsciously, you apply the same framework to your relationship:

- If I plan the vacation, I'm showing up.

- If I pay attention to what they like and deliver it, I'm thoughtful.

- If I fix what they complain about, I'm improving.

- If I don't react emotionally, I'm stable.

In performance environments, that logic is flawless.
In emotional environments, it's deafening.

Your partner doesn't experience your systems — they experience your absence.

Because here's what you didn't account for:
Love isn't linear. It isn't earned through productivity. And it doesn't respond to strategy.

You think you're being reliable.
They feel you're being robotic.

You think you're offering solutions.
They feel you're dodging connection.

You think you're building trust.
They feel they're walking on eggshells — afraid to break your sense of control.

This is the hidden arrogance of success:
You don't question your methods.
Because they work — everywhere else.

But relationships aren't "everywhere else."
They're not projects.
They're not companies.
They're not feedback loops.
They're living, breathing, vulnerable, inconvenient, and emotionally irrational.

And that's not a flaw. That's the point.

Here's where it gets even trickier:

You *know* how to be emotionally available in theory.
You've read the books. You've bookmarked the threads.
You might even be fluent in therapy terms.
But in practice, when your partner brings something raw or unstructured to you,
your nervous system goes into lockdown.

Because it can't be solved.
Because it's not clear.
Because it's not fair.
Because it's not efficient.
Because it doesn't *feel safe.*

And so you default to silence. Or strategy. Or shifting the conversation away from the edge.

That's not emotional maturity. That's emotional muting.

Not because you're emotionally underdeveloped —
but because your performance operating system has no file for "just be with what is."

It knows how to win.
It doesn't know how to *witness*.

If you're still reading, here's the hardest truth in this section:

> **Your partner doesn't want your effort.**
> **They want your *self*.**

Not your plans. Not your goals. Not your schedule.
Not the best version of you.

The you that's willing to be soft, unsure, unpolished —
and present anyway.

Until you dismantle the belief that love is another arena to master,
you will keep performing when your partner is just asking you to be real.

Elon Musk and the Pathology of Performance

Elon Musk is one of the most brilliant minds of the modern era.
A polymath. A visionary. A master builder of systems.

He's reinvented how we think about cars, space, money, energy, AI — and arguably, time itself.
He works 80-hour weeks. Sleeps on factory floors. Makes billion-dollar decisions on four hours of sleep.

But when it comes to intimacy?

He struggles — openly.

He's been divorced three times.
He's spoken publicly about his loneliness.
In one interview, he admitted:
"Being in love hurts a lot. I have a lot of difficulty with that."

Let that land.

The man who is solving interplanetary travel
can't quite solve emotional closeness.

Because even the sharpest mind in the world
can't outthink the nervous system.

This isn't about Elon.
It's about what he *represents* — a cultural archetype:
The Hyperfunctional Man.
The Builder. The Genius. The Savior of Systems.
But emotionally? Lost.

He's the mirror held up to an entire generation of high-
functioning, emotionally malnourished achievers.

Men and women who can master markets but not eye
contact.
Who are fluent in code but mute in conflict.
Who can forecast five years ahead but can't sit with five
minutes of unstructured emotion from someone they love.

Musk is the most extreme version of a very common
pattern:

People who dominate the external world but feel bewildered in the internal one.

This pattern isn't accidental — it's rewarded.

We praise obsession.
We glorify the grind.
We romanticize men who sacrifice everything for their mission.

And then we act surprised when their marriages collapse,
when their kids feel abandoned,
when their partners become "another problem" they don't know how to solve.

We've built a society where emotional incompetence is tolerated — even expected —
if it comes bundled with intelligence, success, and output.

We'll let you be distant, distracted, or emotionally fragile —
as long as you keep building something impressive.

But here's the quiet truth no one wants to say:
Success without emotional fluency breeds loneliness.

The kind of loneliness that no IPO, podcast appearance, or follower count can fix.
The kind that crawls in around 11:38 p.m.,
when the Slack channel is silent,
the lights are off,
and the person in bed next to you feels miles away.

This section isn't meant to vilify Elon Musk.
It's meant to offer a warning.

Because if *he* — with all his intellect, power, and resource — can't automate love, shortcut vulnerability, or solve for intimacy…

Then maybe it's time to stop trying to do the same.

The Mechanics of Misapplication

You didn't become successful by accident.
You developed an operating system: a set of beliefs and strategies that let you dominate in complex environments.

You learned to:

- **Control variables** to reduce risk

- **Predict outcomes** to stay ahead

- **Measure progress** to keep improving

This mindset is powerful. It's what separates performers from spectators.
It's what scaled your company, refined your process, sharpened your edge.

But here's the part nobody tells you:
The very traits that serve you in business can quietly sabotage you in love.

Why?

Because relationships are not mechanical systems.
They are emotional ecosystems.
And ecosystems don't reward force. They respond to presence.

When you apply your success tactics to emotional connection,
you end up using the wrong tools for the right goal.

Let's name them.

The Three False Transfers

1. Control → Emotional Safety

In business, control creates stability.
You reduce uncertainty to reduce exposure. You manage chaos to manage risk.

But in love?
Control suffocates.
Your partner doesn't want to be managed.
They want to be *trusted*.
They want room to change, contradict themselves, cry, erupt, be raw.

Control feels like strategy to you —
but it feels like surveillance to them.

When they say *"I don't feel safe with you,"*
they're not saying they're afraid of you.

They're saying:
"There's no space for me to be messy, spontaneous, or unoptimized — and still loved."

2. Predictability → Presence

You love predictability.
 Forecasts. Models. Morning routines. You built your life around reducing randomness.

In relationships, you use the same logic:
"Let's set expectations."
"Let's define what success looks like."

But love doesn't care about your projections.
 It lives in the unexpected —
 The unplanned moment of eye contact.
 The unguarded laugh.
 The unfiltered emotion.

You can't predict intimacy.
 You have to *feel* it. In real time.
 And if you're always looking one step ahead,
 you're never where they are.

You're optimizing connection out of existence.

3. Measurement → Meaning

In your world, everything gets measured:

- Sales.

- Sleep cycles.

- Step count.

- Conversations per week.

- Frequency of sex.

- Time spent "together."

It feels like accountability.
It feels like intentionality.

But it slowly reduces love to a dashboard.

You start performing relationship tasks instead of inhabiting relationship *truths*.

And eventually, your partner doesn't feel loved.
They feel evaluated.

They don't care how often you text if they don't feel your attention.
They don't care that you booked the dinner if you're on Slack the whole time.

They don't want data. They want depth.

And you can't measure depth.
You can only be in it — or not.

So here's the problem in one sentence:
You're using engineering logic in an emotional arena.

You're trying to make your partner *understand you* the way an investor understands a pitch.
You're trying to make them *trust you* the way a customer trusts a brand.
You're trying to make the relationship *work* the way a system works.

But systems are maintained.
Love is *lived.*

The sooner you see that,
 the sooner you'll stop overperforming and
underconnecting.

And the sooner your partner will finally exhale and say:
 "There you are."

The First Crack in the System

There's a moment — quiet, almost forgettable — that
cracks your operating system.

It's not the fight.
 It's not the affair.
 It's not even the breakup.

It's the stillness after your partner says something simple.
 Something like:
 "You're here, but I don't feel you."

You don't know what to say.
 Not because you don't care — but because you don't
know what "feel" even means in this context.
 You were never taught that language.

You grew up learning to be useful. To win. To outwork,
outmaneuver, outperform.
 And now you're being asked to be something no one ever
rewarded:
 Emotionally present.

This is where the high achiever flinches.
Not because they're cold. But because presence is the one thing they can't master with effort.

You can't schedule it.
You can't study for it.
You can't delegate it, outsource it, or iterate it into being.

You can only show up — and *stay.*

And that terrifies you.
Because presence doesn't offer control.
It offers exposure.

You're not just afraid of intimacy.
You're afraid of being known in a way you don't control.

You've spent your entire life earning love through performance.
But what if the only way to be loved now...
is to stop performing?

This is the crack.

Not a breakdown.
A breakthrough — if you're brave enough to let it widen.

This is the first moment where your logic pauses long enough to hear the truth behind your partner's silence.

Where your systems are suddenly revealed for what they are:
Beautiful, effective, efficient — and emotionally useless.

Where the house you built starts to echo.
Impressive. Structured. Empty.

Here's what you'll want to do now:
Rebuild. Reframe. Solve.

Don't.

Instead:
Let the crack stay open.
Let the discomfort exist.

This isn't where you fix it.
It's where you *stop* fixing it.

Let it be raw. Let it be unfamiliar.

Let this be the first moment in your relationship
where you didn't try to be impressive —
you just tried to be *real*.

~~~~~

*The most important shift in your relationship
isn't something you do.
It's something you stop doing.*

*You stop trying to earn love through effort.
You start receiving it through presence.*

~~~~~

Metrics Without Meaning

Data-Driven Disconnection

He tracks everything.

Morning HRV score.
 Weekly workouts.
 Quarterly financial goals.
 CRM follow-ups.
 Monthly relationship check-ins.
 Number of dinners together.
 Sex frequency (categorized by duration and partner
satisfaction rating — based on post-intimacy survey).

To the outside world, he is what success looks like:
 Stable relationship. Structured routine. A man who invests
in love with the same diligence he brings to work.

To his partner?
 He's become unbearable.

Because while he's quantifying connection, she's starving
for *presence*.
 While he's tweaking the rhythm of their shared life,
 she's quietly asking herself a devastating question:
 "Why do I feel lonelier the more effort he puts in?"

You may not track your relationship in spreadsheets —
 but you probably do it in your head.

You calculate:

● How often you check in.

- How much you provide.

- How frequently you plan dates.

- How rarely you raise your voice.

- How consistently you "show up."

And when your partner says they feel distant from you, you run the numbers.

You replay the week:
We had dinner Tuesday.
I was present during that movie.
I texted them at lunch.
We had sex Friday.

You review your effort like a ledger.

Because in your mind, emotional connection is an output. And effort always equals value.

Except here's the truth you've been avoiding:
Connection isn't a number. It's a nervous system experience.

Your partner doesn't feel your effort.
They feel your energy.
Your orientation.
Your availability.
Your *aliveness* in the moment.

And if all they're getting is your structure, your reliability, your performance —
but never your raw, unfiltered attention —
they will begin to disappear in plain sight.

This is the emotional starvation of the modern high-functioning relationship:
Effort is present. Emotion is absent.

There's conversation, but no depth.
There's sex, but no electricity.
There's routine, but no mystery.

You're doing everything right —
except the thing that matters most.

Not because you don't care.
But because you're mistaking your metrics for meaning.

You've built a relationship you can *track*.
But can you feel it?

Can they?

The real problem isn't that you're disconnected.
It's that you've been performing connection —
without ever noticing that your partner stopped believing it.

They don't want your dashboard.
They want you.

And if you don't realize that soon,
you'll find yourself holding a perfectly optimized relationship…
with no one left inside it.

The Quantification of Intimacy

High performers trust numbers.
 Not just because they're measurable — but because they're controllable.

Numbers don't argue.
 They don't change their mind in the middle of a sentence.
 They don't cry.
 They don't ask you to slow down and *feel*.

Numbers are safe.
 People aren't.

Which is why, when your relationship starts to feel uncertain,
 you reach for the closest tool you know: **measurement.**

You start tracking how often you talk.
 You schedule "intentional quality time."
 You set goals for intimacy.
 You evaluate progress.
 You define what "success" in the relationship looks like.

All of it sounds smart.
 All of it *feels* like love.

It's not.

It's **control in disguise.**

Here's the truth:
 You're not measuring intimacy. You're performing accountability.

You're using metrics to prove — mostly to yourself — that you're doing a good job.
But love isn't a job.
It's not earned by frequency or optimized through routine.
It's not a set of inputs that yield predictable outputs.

It's a dynamic, irrational, emotional ecosystem.
And ecosystems die when you try to manage them like a supply chain.

You don't strengthen connection by tightening the system.
You do it by loosening your grip.

Because presence isn't trackable.
Safety isn't quantifiable.
Trust doesn't care how many hours you logged together this week —
only how real you were during the five minutes they needed you most.

This is the danger of living in metrics:
You begin to value the visible over the meaningful.

A perfectly timed text becomes more important than a heartfelt pause.
A consistent dinner routine becomes more impressive than shared laughter.
A detailed plan becomes a substitute for vulnerability.

And slowly, without knowing it,
you start building a relationship that *looks* healthy —
but feels hollow.

You're hitting your numbers.
You're on top of your routines.
You're doing everything a "great partner" should.

But your partner doesn't feel you.
Because you're not there.
You're in the system.
Not the moment.

You think your structure is showing love.
They feel like you're hiding behind it.

Because here's the truth no spreadsheet will show you:

Presence can't be faked.
And intimacy can't be tracked.

The second you turn your relationship into a checklist,
you stop living it —
and start managing it.

And no one wants to be managed in love.

Tim Ferriss and the Quantified Self

Tim Ferriss didn't just popularize life optimization — he
turned it into an art form.

With *The 4-Hour Workweek*, he gave a generation of high
performers permission to systematize their lives.
Time, travel, income, fitness, reading — everything could
be streamlined.
Everything could be tracked.
Everything could be *hacked*.

And it worked.

For millions of people, Ferriss was the gateway drug to better habits, sharper thinking, and unprecedented control over their daily experience.

But hidden inside his empire of mastery is a quiet confession.
A sentence most of his fans miss.
One he repeats in different forms across interviews, podcasts, and pages.

> *"The better I got at optimizing, the harder it became to feel."*

This is not a failure of Ferriss.
It's the shadow of the mindset he helped pioneer:
the Quantified Self.

The idea that if you can track it, you can master it.
And if you can master it, you can be safe.

But emotional life doesn't play by those rules.
It doesn't get clearer the more you analyze it.
It doesn't become manageable the more you dissect it.

In fact, the more you try to measure it —
the more it vanishes.

Ferriss has admitted to periods of depression, isolation, and intense disconnection.
He's spoken about struggling to feel alive even when everything was working on paper.

And he's not alone.
Behind many of the world's most "optimized" lives
are people who quietly wonder why intimacy feels like a
foreign language
— and why they're still lonely.

Because emotional reality isn't a tech stack.
It's not about refining inputs.
It's about tolerating ambiguity. Sitting in discomfort.
Staying when there's nothing to fix.

And that's the muscle optimization doesn't train.
That's the muscle success often forgets.

This is where the Quantified Self hits its limit:

- You can optimize your body, but not your partner's
  tone of voice.

- You can track your sleep, but not the moment your
  relationship stops feeling safe.

- You can A/B test your routines, but not your
  emotional availability.

Love doesn't yield to life design.
It doesn't respond to improvement.
It responds to presence.

And presence is *inefficient*.

It's messy. It's slow. It doesn't scale.

But it's the one thing your partner actually wants.

So yes, you can learn from Tim Ferriss.
But also learn *what he had to unlearn*:
That mastery without meaning is a trap.
And that even the sharpest minds eventually have to confront
the one part of life they can't optimize into submission:
real emotional connection.

What Can't Be Counted

You know how to measure progress.
That's how you've survived.
That's how you've won.

Show you a metric, and you'll improve it.
Give you a target, and you'll hit it.
Tell you how success is defined, and you'll outperform expectations.

But what happens when the thing that matters most
can't be measured at all?

What happens when the most critical moments in your relationship —
the ones that decide trust, safety, attraction, longevity —
don't show up on a chart?

Here's what doesn't show up in your dashboard:

- The half-second of hesitation in your partner's voice

- The warmth in your eyes when you're not trying to prove anything

- The stillness between breaths, when neither of you is talking

- The unconscious way they turn toward you — or away — when they walk in the room

- The way your body tenses when you're listening to *fix*, not to feel

These are the real signals of intimacy.
They're subtle. Irrational. Impossible to optimize.
But they're everything.

They determine whether your partner feels emotionally safe —
or quietly anxious.
Connected — or alone.
Loved — or tolerated.

You'll never be able to chart that.
But your partner *feels it immediately*.

This is where the optimization mindset collapses.
Because it assumes that value is proportional to clarity.
That the more measurable something is, the more meaningful it becomes.

But love flips that on its head.

The things that matter most can't be counted.

- You can't track presence.

- You can't quantify attunement.

- You can't measure trust with a weekly report.

- You can't score the feeling of being *fully received* by someone who isn't trying to fix you.

High performers hate this.
Because it means you can't *earn* intimacy the way you earned success.
You have to *surrender* to it.

It also means you can't know if you're doing it right.
You can only feel your way into it — moment by moment — without certainty, feedback, or control.

That's not inefficient.
That's human.

And the longer you avoid that, the longer you'll stay emotionally adjacent to your relationship —
 close enough to manage it,
 but never close enough to live inside it.

What makes love meaningful is exactly what makes it untrackable:

> **It happens in the space between signals —
> in the quiet, in the unknown, in the
> moment you stop trying to prove you're
> good at it.**

The second you try to measure it,
 you're already outside of it.

Presence Is Not a Metric

You can feel it the moment it happens.

Your partner is speaking — but you're not really there.
 You're thinking about how to respond, how to help, how to
protect your image.
 You're calculating the emotional cost of what they're
saying
 instead of absorbing the emotional truth behind it.

You're present in body, but your nervous system is still
scanning for strategy.

Because even here — in this soft, vulnerable space —
 you're still trying to *win*.

Still trying to be good.
 Still trying to get it right.
 Still trying to offer proof:
 Look how much I'm trying.
 Look at how I show up.
 Look at everything I do.

But love doesn't care about your proof.
 It cares about your presence.

And presence is not something you can *do*.
 It's not something you can plan for or measure or grade.

It's something you become.
 Or you don't.

Here's what presence actually means:
 It means you're not bracing.
 You're not performing.
 You're not holding your breath, waiting to explain yourself
or fix the discomfort.

It means your partner can break down, and you don't
move.
 You don't flinch. You don't leave — emotionally or
mentally.

It means you're not tracking the clock.
 You're not scanning for solutions.
 You're not benchmarking this moment against your past
performance.

You're just there.

Feeling them. Feeling yourself.
 In all your unpolished, unfixed, unoptimized humanity.

And that's the one thing they've been asking for all along.

You want to be good at love.
 That desire is real.
 But if you keep trying to be *good at it*,
 you'll miss what it actually requires:

Not skill. Not structure. Not effort.
 But contact. Emotional contact.

And emotional contact requires your presence — not your
resume.

It doesn't matter how many boxes you check.
If your partner doesn't feel your availability,
your effort will feel empty.

Not because you're not trying —
but because you're trying in the wrong direction.

You don't need to stop being excellent.
You need to stop turning love into a project.

You don't need to lower your standards.
You need to abandon the illusion that love is something
you can *optimize.*

And you don't need to "work on the relationship."
You need to step *into* it — unguarded, unmeasured,
unperfected.

Because the moment you stop calculating...
is the moment you finally arrive.

~~~~

Presence is not a metric.
It's not something you score.
It's something you feel.
And until you stop trying to prove you're
present,
you never really will be.

~~~~

Love Isn't a KPI

Effort ≠ Intimacy

He doesn't understand.

He plans the vacations.
 He pays attention to what she likes.
 He sends thoughtful gifts.
 He remembers dates.
 He shows up for her events — even the ones he finds
boring.
 He doesn't yell. He doesn't cheat. He doesn't disappear.

And yet — she's pulling away.

She says she feels "alone with him."
 That he's "checked out emotionally."
 That she can't feel his presence — just his performance.

He's stunned.
 Because in his mind, he's a *model partner.*
 He gives. He shows up. He tries.

But that's the problem:
 He thinks effort equals intimacy.

You might be him.

You do all the right things.
 You stay faithful. You ask questions. You support their
dreams.
 You try to be better.
 And it's not fake — you mean it. You care.

But they keep saying things like:

- *"You're not listening."*

- *"I don't feel like we're connected."*

- *"You're here, but you're not here."*

It doesn't compute.

Because in your world, doing equals caring.
Effort equals value.
Showing up equals presence.

But relationships don't obey that logic.

Effort is visible.
Intimacy is felt.

You can do everything "right" and still not be received.
Because your partner doesn't want your checklist.
They want *you*.

Here's what makes this so disorienting for high performers:
You were taught to *act* your values.
To demonstrate care through consistency, competence,
and discipline.

That works in leadership.
It works in personal branding.
It works in public.

But it falls apart in love.

Because love doesn't respond to effort — it responds to **emotional contact**.
And emotional contact is not about what you do.
It's about *how you're being*.

You can spend the day together and still feel miles apart.
You can sit across from your partner and never actually *reach* them.
You can hold their hand and never *let them feel you.*

Because you're not in the moment —
you're managing the moment.

You're thinking about doing it right.
Not about being real.

This is where so many high achievers quietly unravel:

They believe they're giving their best —
but they've never actually given their **emotional self.**

They're performing love
instead of participating in it.

And performance, no matter how sincere,
always creates distance.
Because it has an audience.
And your partner can feel when you're performing for them
instead of simply being with them.

The worst part?
You're exhausted from trying.
You've been showing up, giving more, adjusting, refining

—
only to hear: *"You're still not here with me."*

It feels like failure.
But it's not.

It's the moment right before a shift —
where you realize that **more effort won't fix this**.

Only *more honesty*, more *presence*, and more *emotional risk* will.

~~~~~

You don't need to do more.
You need to stop hiding behind what you do.

~~~~~

The KPI Illusion

You treat your relationship like you treat everything else that matters:
You define success.
You put in the reps.
You track progress.
You expect results.

And when something feels off, you ask yourself:

- *Am I doing enough?*

- *Am I meeting expectations?*

- *Am I showing up consistently?*

These are great questions — if you're running a team.

But in a relationship?
They miss the point entirely.

Because connection doesn't operate like a business unit.
And love doesn't follow performance logic.

A **KPI**, in your world, is a *Key Performance Indicator.*
It helps you measure success.
It's precise. Trackable. Motivating.

So it makes sense that you'd bring that same framework into your relationship.
You start to think of love in deliverables:

- Number of meaningful conversations per week

- Frequency of sex

- Quality of conflict resolution

- Expressions of gratitude

- Shared goals

- Time together logged

From the outside, it looks intentional.
Responsible. Emotionally literate.

But under the surface, you're still running a system that asks:
"How do I win this?"

And love doesn't want to be won.
It wants to be lived.
Felt. Witnessed. Held.

Here's what makes the KPI illusion so seductive:
It gives you *structure* in a place that feels unpredictable.
It lets you focus on *what you're doing*
so you don't have to feel *what you're missing*.

When your partner seems dissatisfied, you review your actions:

- "I planned the dinner."

- "I asked about their day."

- "I said I loved them before bed."

- "We talked about this already — didn't we?"

But what you're really doing
is pulling data to defend a reality your partner doesn't feel.

You're arguing for effort —
when what they want is *your presence*.

You're optimizing performance —
when what they need is *emotional contact.*

And no metric, no matter how well-intentioned,
can replace that.

This is the cost of using KPIs in love:
You start treating your partner like a client.
You start treating connection like a deliverable.
You start managing feedback instead of listening for pain.

Eventually, your relationship becomes a company culture
review.
Safe. Structured. Respectful.
And emotionally flat.

You're doing everything right —
except the one thing that matters:
letting go of the system.

Your partner doesn't want to be a stakeholder in your
emotional growth plan.
They want to feel you.

Not your process.
Not your outline.
Not your performance.

Just *you.*
Raw. Real. Without a scorecard.

~~~~~

*The moment you start tracking love,
you stop trusting it.*

~~~~~

Jeff Bezos and the Cost of Achievement

Jeff Bezos is one of the most successful individuals of our time.

He scaled a business into a global empire.
 He turned logistics into an art form.
 He's redefined how the modern world consumes, works, and even dreams.

And along the way, he lost his marriage.

The headlines were polite.
 They used words like "amicable" and "respectful."
 But the subtext was deafening:
 **Even the most structured, high-performing life
 can quietly erode what matters most.**

This isn't a criticism of Bezos.
 It's a reflection of a larger truth —
 the emotional cost of scale.

Bezos didn't fail at love because he didn't care.
 He failed because he was moving at the speed of ambition,
 and intimacy moves slower than that.

Love doesn't scale.
It doesn't automate.
It doesn't yield to efficiency.
And it certainly doesn't care how many zeros are in your net worth.

It cares whether you can sit still,
look into someone else's eyes,
and say, without flinching:
"I'm still here."

Not just physically — but emotionally, relationally, energetically.

And when your world is built around winning, expanding, optimizing, and dominating,
that kind of stillness can feel like death.

What Bezos represents isn't failure.
He represents **the cultural ideal taken to its logical conclusion**:

- Scale everything

- Win everything

- Optimize everything

- Outsource everything

But love can't be scaled.
And intimacy doesn't survive delegation.

If you've spent your life building something massive,
 you know what it takes:
 Time. Presence. Obsession. Tradeoffs.

Now ask yourself:
 What have you been trading intimacy for?

Freedom? Security? Achievement?
 The high of forward motion?

And are you willing to admit
 that you may have been **winning at the wrong thing**?

Bezos didn't stop being a visionary.
 He just outgrew the relational structure that existed before
he realized
 how deeply human connection resists *systems thinking*.

And many high performers will face this same reckoning —
 not in scandal, but in silence.

In the quiet distance between themselves and the person
beside them.
 In the "everything's fine" dinner conversations.
 In the creeping ache that nothing is *wrong*,
 but something is no longer *alive*.

This section is not about billionaires.
 It's about you.

The part of you that believes if you just *do enough*, provide
enough, prove enough —
 your partner will feel it.

But effort without attunement isn't love.
It's shadow work.
It's control wrapped in generosity.
It's a performance with excellent production values
and no emotional core.

~~~~~

If your success outgrows your intimacy,
you're not building a life — you're leaving one
behind.

~~~~~

The Spectacle of Showing Up

You show up.
You're present.
You do the things a good partner does.

You post the anniversary photo.
You write the thoughtful caption.
You plan the trip.
You say the words.

From the outside, it looks perfect.

You are "the partner who shows up."
You're the one who puts in the effort.
You're the one who reads the relationship books, has the
couples therapist on speed dial, and schedules intentional
time together.

You've built a brand of emotional competence.

And your partner is still starving.

This is the danger of modern self-awareness:
It can become performance just like anything else.

You're not faking.
But you're still curating.

You've taken what should be intimate
and turned it into a kind of presentation —
not for strangers, but for your partner.
And over time, they start to feel like your audience.

Because underneath your care
is still a desire to be *seen as caring*.
Underneath your presence
is still a desire to be *acknowledged for showing up*.

You're still performing love.
Just with better lighting.

High performers are masters of this.
You've trained your entire life to earn validation
through showing the right signals.

But intimacy doesn't speak in signals.
It speaks in *resonance*.
It doesn't respond to how much you give —
but to how much of you is *actually there* when you give it.

And when your love becomes a series of gestures
 instead of a state of being,
 your partner can feel it.

They might not have the words,
 but they know something's missing.
 They know your hand is on theirs —
 but your mind is three rooms away, planning tomorrow.

They know you said all the right things —
 but none of it landed.

Because love isn't a speech.
 It's a pulse.
 And they can tell when yours is gone.

You've mistaken showing up for *being in it*.
 You've mistaken consistency for connection.
 You've mistaken demonstration for devotion.

You've built a *spectacle of effort* —
 and your partner is the only one who knows the
difference.

And here's the painful truth:

> **It doesn't matter what you do
> if none of it makes them feel close to you.**

Because proximity isn't presence.
 Effort isn't intimacy.
 And optics are not love.

~~~~~

When connection becomes a performance,
your partner stops clapping —
and starts quietly walking away.

~~~~~

Love Is a Mirror, Not a Metric

Love doesn't care how hard you tried.
It cares how you made them feel.

Not what you did.
Not how consistent you were.
Not how well you executed the anniversary weekend or remembered the coffee order.

How you made them feel.
That's it.

And that's the part you can't control.
Because how someone feels around you
isn't a product of your effort.
It's a reflection of your energy, your truth, your availability.

Love is a mirror.

It doesn't reflect your intentions.
It reflects your presence.

This is what high performers often miss:
You think love is something you *achieve*.
It's not.

Love isn't impressed.
It's *informed*.

By your attention.
By your safety.
By your emotional honesty.
By how much of you is actually there when it matters.

You want to know if your relationship is healthy?
Look at your partner's nervous system.

Not their words.
Not their gratitude.
Not their praise for how "present" you are.
Look at how they relax — or tense — around you.
Look at whether they shrink or expand in your presence.
Look at how often they reach for you — or retreat.

That's the metric you've been missing.
Not performance.
Impact.

So ask yourself:

- Does my partner feel safer when I enter the room
  — or when I leave it?

- Do they feel loved — or managed?

- Do they feel seen — or scanned?

- Do they feel emotionally free — or emotionally obligated?

Because love isn't a review of your output.
 It's a reflection of who you are when you're *not trying to perform.*

And if the mirror keeps showing you disconnection,
 the answer isn't to work harder.
 It's to ask a better question:

Who am I being in this moment?
 And is that version of me capable of connection — or just performance?

This is where intimacy begins:
 Not with more effort.
 Not with more structure.
 But with a brutal kind of honesty:

> *If you're still keeping score, you're still performing.*
> *And if you're still performing,*
> *you're not inside the relationship — you're outside it,*
> *trying to manage what should be lived.*

Love isn't a KPI.
 It's a mirror.

And it's time you stopped polishing your metrics
 and started facing your reflection.

Why Logic Loses in Love

The Problem Solver's Blind Spot

She's crying again.
 Not in a dramatic way. Not loud. Just quietly, almost like she's apologizing for it.

He doesn't raise his voice.
 He doesn't get defensive.
 He waits for her to finish, then calmly asks,
 "Can you help me understand what you're actually upset about?"

He thinks this is empathy.
 She feels like she's talking to a customer service chatbot.

You've probably done this too.

Your partner is in pain — emotionally overwhelmed, triggered, spiraling —
 and you stay calm. Measured. Rational.

You wait for a clear signal.
 You look for a root cause.
 You try to isolate the problem.

You're proud of yourself for not reacting.
 You think staying grounded is helpful. Mature.

But what your partner experiences is something else entirely:
 distance.
 disconnection.

**and worst of all — being intellectually observed
instead of emotionally met.**

You were taught to solve problems.
It's how you became successful.
It's how you protect your team, your company, your
identity.

But love isn't a problem to solve.
And when you treat it like one,
you turn pain into data
and vulnerability into a puzzle.

Your partner doesn't want a diagnosis.
They want a *witness*.

They want to know that their feelings don't scare you.
That they can unravel and still be held.
That you don't need to understand it in order to stay.

And every time you interrupt their pain with logic —
even with good intentions —
you prove one thing:

> *You care more about resolving the moment
> than connecting in it.*

This is the blind spot:
You confuse calm with love.
You confuse clarity with compassion.
You confuse understanding with intimacy.

You're so busy trying to decode what they mean
that you miss what they're actually asking for:
"Can I show you how I feel... and will you stay?"

But you don't hear that.
You hear a system breaking down.
You feel the urge to fix it — now.

And that's where it all goes wrong.

When you solve too soon,
you silence the very thing they need you to hear.

When you respond too cleanly,
you signal that emotion is inefficient.

And when you stay in your head
while they're drowning in feeling,
you confirm their worst fear:
"I'm too much. Even for you."

The blind spot isn't that you don't care.
It's that your care is filtered through cognition — not
connection.
And no one feels held when they're being analyzed.

~~~~

You're not being rational.
You're being emotionally unavailable —
just with better vocabulary.

~~~~

The Myth of Rational Clarity

You want things to make sense.

You're not afraid of emotion — as long as it's coherent.
If your partner can explain why they're upset, what it
connects to, and what they need,
you're all in.

But when the emotion is chaotic?
When the logic breaks down?
When the feeling arrives without a thesis?

You freeze.
Or worse — you start asking questions:

- *"What exactly are you trying to say?"*

- *"Can we slow down and break this down?"*

- *"But last week, you said the opposite…"*

You think you're helping.
But what you're really doing is trying to steer the moment
back into territory where you feel safe.

Because *emotion without clarity* threatens the system you
live by.

High performers worship clarity.
It's what makes you decisive.
Efficient. Trustworthy.
It's what makes people want to follow you.

But here's the problem:
Love is not built on clarity.
It's built on presence.

And presence doesn't always make sense.

Sometimes your partner contradicts themselves.
 Sometimes they feel two things at once.
 Sometimes they don't *know* what they need.
 Sometimes they just want to fall apart — without a
narrative, without a plan, without a point.

That doesn't make them unstable.
 It makes them *human.*

This is the myth of rational clarity:
That understanding precedes connection.

It doesn't.

You don't need to understand someone to hold them.
 You don't need to trace their logic to validate their pain.
 You don't need to make sense of the moment to stay
inside it.

You just have to *stop demanding coherence*
 from a part of life that isn't supposed to be coherent.

This is what love asks of you:
 Let go of your need to make it neat.
 To fix the contradiction.
 To reach a conclusion.

There is no conclusion.

Just a heartbeat, a body, a presence —
inviting you to stop thinking
and start *feeling with*.

If you want real intimacy,
you have to accept this:

> *Love is not logical.*
> *It is messy.*
> *And the more you try to make it make sense,*
> *the more you make your partner feel like*
> *they're not allowed to be fully human.*

Naval Ravikant and the Stoic Disconnect

Naval Ravikant is the archetype of modern clarity.

He's built wealth, credibility, and an entire school of
thought around one central premise:
a well-lived life is a well-designed one.

His ideas are lean, disciplined, powerful:

- Happiness is a skill.

- Avoid unnecessary suffering.

- Master your desires.

- Choose peace over chaos.

- Protect your energy.

- Don't argue. Walk away.

On paper, it's brilliant.
Online, it's gospel.

But behind the Stoic serenity is a subtle fracture —
the same fracture found in boardrooms, investor retreats,
meditation pods, and perfectly optimized lives.

A private struggle with *intimacy*.

Naval has spoken candidly about love and connection.
In interviews, he's reflected on breakups, identity loss,
avoidance of conflict, and the difficulty of letting someone
else's chaos into his world.

He's said:

> *"If you're truly peaceful and happy, you'll have
> very few relationships."*

It's a powerful line — and a revealing one.

Because it points to the unspoken assumption of the stoic
achiever:
That love, emotion, and closeness are risks to peace.
That other people's intensity is a threat to your clarity.
That conflict is distraction.
That needs are noise.

And once you believe that,
 you start to mistake *emotional distance* for *emotional mastery.*

This is the Stoic Disconnect:
 You think you're evolved —
 but really, you're just alone.

You think you've transcended need —
 but really, you've just built a world where no one gets close enough to need you.

You think you're being unreactive —
 but really, you're unresponsive.
 Unavailable.
 Unreachable.

This is not an attack on Naval.
 It's a spotlight on the cultural pattern he embodies.

He is not the villain.
 He is the mirror.

A mirror for the emotionally intelligent thinker
 who remains fundamentally unavailable in love.

A mirror for the man (or woman) who can distill wisdom into one-liners
 but can't sit through five minutes of their partner's raw, messy, illogical sadness.

A mirror for the brilliant, inwardly regulated, high-performing person

who has no idea how much of their "peace"
is actually just *emotional avoidance, dressed in robes.*

Intimacy isn't a breach of your self-mastery.
It's the *proof* of it.

Because real mastery isn't how little something affects you.
It's how deeply you can *let it in* — and stay.

That's what the Stoic system can't teach you:
**how to let someone into your stillness
without turning them into a threat.**

~~~~~

> If your peace can't survive someone else's
> pain,
> it's not peace.
> It's insulation.

~~~~~

The Fear Beneath Fixing

You think you're helping.
When your partner breaks down, spirals, lashes out —
you stay calm. You ask clarifying questions.
You search for what can be improved.

But that's not love.
That's self-protection.

Fixing gives you something to do
so you don't have to feel helpless.

Because underneath all your logic,
beneath the patience, the posture, the self-control,
is a deep, primal fear:

What if I can't do anything to make this better?

And if that's true —
if there's no solution,
no fix,
no framework —
then you have to sit in the one place that terrifies you
most:
powerless,
present,
and fully emotionally exposed.

This is what high performers almost never admit:

You don't solve because you care.
You solve because you're afraid.

Afraid that if you don't do something, you'll fail.
Afraid that if you stay in the mess, it'll consume you.
Afraid that if you show how lost you feel, you'll lose
control.

So you grip the one tool you know how to wield — your
mind.
You intellectualize. You reframe. You redirect.
You package their pain into a narrative.
You shrink it down into something you can hold.

But they don't want it held.
They want it *felt with*.

They want you —
raw, messy, unknowing.
Not because you'll fix it.
But because you *won't leave them alone in it.*

Fixing is not love.
Fixing is control in a suit.

It makes you feel strong.
Useful. Essential.
But it disconnects you from the one thing that actually matters in love:
your emotional availability.

Because real intimacy isn't when you do something *about* the pain.
It's when you let the pain be there
without running from it, reorganizing it, or shutting it down.

This is where love asks you to surrender:
Not by becoming less competent —
but by finally admitting that some things can't be optimized.
Some moments can't be led.
Some emotions don't need to be managed — they need to be shared.

And that sharing, that soft, terrifying, unsolvable sharing —
is what love has been asking for from you this entire time.

~~~~

You don't fix because you're strong.
 You fix because you're afraid to feel
powerless.
 But your power isn't in solving.
 It's in staying.

~~~~

Let the Problem Exist

You've been taught to take action.

In your world, inaction is negligence.
 Problems don't sit — they get solved.
 Silence is failure.
 Passivity is weakness.
 You do. You move. You lead.

But love doesn't always want a leader.
 Sometimes, it wants a witness.

And sometimes the most powerful thing you can do
 is nothing.

Just let the pain sit in the room.
 Let the anger breathe.
 Let the confusion stay unnamed.

Let the problem exist.

This doesn't mean detachment.
This doesn't mean backing away or "letting them figure it out."

It means:
Stop trying to fix what was never yours to control in the first place.

Let them cry without organizing their words.
Let them vent without redirecting their logic.
Let them contradict themselves without holding them to yesterday's clarity.

Let the discomfort stay uncomfortable.

That's what love asks of you — not because it's passive, but because it's real.

Presence is not passive.
It is the most active form of restraint.

To not rescue.
To not manage.
To not shrink someone's pain into something more digestible for you.

To just be there.
Unguarded. Silent. Breathing.

That's love.

Not the clean kind.
Not the performative kind.
The kind that makes your chest hurt

because you're no longer in control
but you're *still choosing to stay.*

Here's what happens when you stop fixing:

Something in them softens.
 They stop defending.
 They start unfolding.

Because for the first time, you're not trying to move the
moment somewhere else.
 You're not trying to prove you're good.
 You're not trying to earn love by doing.

You're just being.
 In the pain.
 With them.

No logic.
 No ladder out.
 No point.

Just presence.

You think your strength is in your mind.
 And it is — in the world.

But in love?
 Your strength is your capacity to stay present without
needing resolution.

And your partner doesn't want you to be perfect.
They want to know that when things fall apart —
you won't.

~~~~~

You don't need to fix it.
You need to feel it — and stay.

Because that's what love really is:
not resolution.
But presence in the unresolved.

~~~~~

Control, Certainty, and Other Intimacy Killers

The Tyrant at Home

He doesn't yell.
He doesn't cheat.
He doesn't leave messes or miss anniversaries.

He plans everything.
He books the restaurant. He checks the reviews. He orders the car early.
He builds the vacation itinerary like it's a launch sequence: Downtime at 9. Activity at 10. "Unstructured connection" penciled in by noon.

He calls it thoughtfulness.
She calls it something else: *exhausting.*

Because every detail is managed.
Every decision goes through him.
Every emotional moment becomes a project he wants to "handle better next time."

And slowly, without realizing it, she stops breathing inside the relationship.

Not out of fear — but out of **restriction**.

Control doesn't always look like abuse.
Sometimes it looks like *competence with edges.*
Like planning everything "for both of you" but never asking what she actually wanted.
Like over-communication that leaves no room for

spontaneity.
 Like hyper-responsibility that quietly erases someone else's freedom.

This is the tyranny of the high-functioning partner:
 you never hurt them on purpose —
 but you make it impossible for them to just *be*.

You think you're protecting the relationship.
 But what you're really doing is protecting *your nervous system*.
 From mess. From ambiguity. From risk.

And while your systems may keep the chaos out,
 they also keep out the intimacy.

Because intimacy can't breathe in a room where everything is managed.
 It needs uncertainty.
 Surprise.
 Disruption.
 Silence.
 Discomfort.
 Emotional honesty without structure.

It needs moments where no one is in charge — and you stay anyway.

If your partner always has to wait for your approval
 before making a decision...
 If they flinch when their emotions don't "fit" into your plan...
 If they stop bringing things up because they know you'll steer the conversation...

Then you're not building connection.
You're building **compliance**.

And compliance doesn't create love.
It creates quiet resentment.
Until one day, they stop showing you who they are —
because it doesn't feel safe to be unpredictable anymore.

You're not a bad person.
You're not malicious.
You're just trying to reduce uncertainty —
because uncertainty makes you feel unsafe.

But love isn't a supply chain.
It's not a workflow.
It's not a protocol.

It's a field of *shared unknowns*.

And if you can't tolerate being out of control,
you'll never fully touch the person standing right in front of
you.

~~~~~

You don't have to be loud to be controlling.
You just have to create a world
where your partner stops breathing freely.

~~~~~

The Cult of Control

You probably don't think of yourself as controlling.
 You're not reactive. You don't micromanage.
 You let your partner have space — as long as it doesn't
affect your rhythm.
 You don't dominate.
 You *guide*.

But control isn't just about volume.
 It's about **prevention**.

Control is what you use to stay ahead of chaos.
 To manage outcomes before they unfold.
 To protect what feels vulnerable
 by keeping everything *predictable, stable, safe.*

And it works — in business.
 In performance.
 In leadership.
 Control creates reliability.

But in love?

Control kills aliveness.

You think you're creating safety.
 But it's safety for *you.*
 Not for them.

You set the tone.
 You set the schedule.
 You track the emotional climate.
 You monitor the tension in the room and course-correct as
needed.

You think this makes you emotionally intelligent.

But what it really does is send one quiet message over and over:

> *"This space needs to stay manageable.*
> *Please don't make me uncomfortable."*

Control isn't always power.
Often, it's fear dressed as competence.

You're not trying to dominate.
You're trying to avoid being overwhelmed.

You were never taught how to sit in chaos.
So you overcompensate by making your relationship low-risk.
You preempt hurt by managing emotions.
You predict your partner's needs so they never get the chance to surprise you.

You eliminate uncertainty —
and along with it,
you eliminate the freedom that love needs to breathe.

Here's what the cult of control never tells you:

- The more stable you make everything,
  the less emotionally flexible you become.

- The more structure you impose,
  the more fragile the connection becomes when

something breaks.

- The more you expect your partner to fit within your system,
  the more they will feel like they're performing for your approval —
  not showing up as themselves.

Control feels safe.
 But it's not love.
 It's a contract: *I will love you as long as you don't disrupt my sense of order.*

And whether you say it out loud or not,
 your partner will feel it.

They'll sense your limits.
 They'll sense your rigidity.
 They'll sense your need for everything to be emotionally tidy —
 and they'll learn not to bring you the parts of themselves that aren't.

And that's how love quietly disappears —
 not in anger, but in accommodation.

~~~~~

Control doesn't make love stronger.
It just makes it quieter —
until one day, there's nothing left to control.

~~~~~

Steve Jobs and the Intolerable Standard

Steve Jobs wasn't just brilliant.
He was obsessive.

Design, detail, perfection — he demanded excellence from
everything around him.
He created products that changed the world,
because he refused to accept anything less than
extraordinary.

And he applied the same mindset to the people in his life.

If they couldn't meet the standard —
he cut them out.

Not maliciously.
Not violently.
But with cold clarity: *"You're not ready. You don't get it."*

To him, love without precision was sentimentality.
Mediocrity. A waste of time.

In business, this obsession made him legendary.
In his personal life — it left scars.

His daughter, Lisa Brennan-Jobs, writes in her memoir
about growing up around his brilliance:
how he made her feel special one day, and invisible the
next.
How his mood shaped the room.
How nothing was ever *quite good enough* — including her.

Jobs could create magic.
 But only if the conditions were perfect.
 And in love, those conditions never are.

This is what happens when high standards become the
only language you know:
 **you start demanding excellence
 from something that was never meant to be perfect.**

You start grading connection.
 Correcting tone.
 Noticing flaws in your partner's timing, language, logic.
 You start managing their expression the way you manage
your brand.

You don't mean to hurt them.
 You just can't help needing everything to meet your level.

But love isn't a pitch deck.
 It doesn't thrive under critique.
 It shrinks under it.

If your partner always feels like they're being evaluated —
 they will stop expressing anything that isn't fully polished.

And slowly, the emotional rawness between you
disappears.
 You're left with something that looks beautiful, sounds
smart, and functions smoothly —
 but has no *aliveness* in it.

Just performance.
 Just silence.

Just the cold ache of being admired but never truly accepted.

This is the intolerable standard:
 The belief that your partner should rise to your level —
 instead of trusting that intimacy happens when you *both* drop the performance.

Jobs was a genius.
 But even genius has limits.
 He could change the world —
 but not without wounding people along the way.

The lesson isn't to be less brilliant.
 It's to stop using your brilliance as a shield against emotional mess.

Because sometimes your greatest strength in the world
 is the very thing making you unbearable to love.

~~~~~

Excellence may earn you respect.
 But only softness will earn you intimacy.

~~~~~

Love and the Unknown

Love is not a system.

It doesn't follow rules.
 It doesn't deliver predictable outputs.

It doesn't reward consistency the way your performance environments do.

And the sooner you accept that,
 the sooner your relationship can start to breathe.

Control is seductive because it gives you the illusion of safety.
 When things feel raw or volatile, you reach for order —
 because *you think you're protecting the relationship.*

But you're not protecting it.
 You're *flattening* it.
 You're sanding down the edges of intimacy until nothing unexpected can get in —
 which also means nothing *real* can either.

Because love lives in the **unknown.**
 It *needs* it.

It needs the messy, unscheduled confession.
 The awkward silence that goes unfilled.
 The conversation you weren't ready for.
 The way your partner surprises you with pain you didn't cause — and still asks you to hold.

The more you fear uncertainty,
 the more you'll try to shape your relationship into something you can manage.

You'll overplan.
 You'll preempt.
 You'll assign meaning to things before your partner

finishes speaking.
 You'll build structure to avoid surrender.

And your partner — even if they can't name it — will feel
your rigidity.
 They'll stop bringing you the unpredictable.
 They'll stop saying what they really feel.
 They'll start curating their truth to protect your sense of
order.

And that's how closeness dies.
 Not with betrayal —
 but with **over-management**.

Love is not something you conquer.
 It's something you step into —
 knowing you will get disoriented.
 Knowing you will lose footing.
 Knowing you cannot predict what will happen next.

But staying anyway.

Staying with the tension.
 Staying when you don't know what they need.
 Staying when nothing makes sense, and everything feels
unfamiliar.

That's where connection lives:
 In the emotional free fall you keep trying to avoid.

You've built your life to minimize risk.
 But love is not a low-risk asset.
 It's volatility in the most beautiful form —

and you don't get the reward unless you *stop bracing for the crash.*

~~~~~

Intimacy isn't built on what you know.
It's built on what you're willing to feel
without needing to make sense of it first.

~~~~~

The Softest Power Is Trust

You think your strength is in your structure.
Your ability to anticipate.
To plan. To deliver. To stay one step ahead.

That's how you keep people safe.
That's how you stay safe.
That's how you've built a life no one else could.

But the truth is this:
In love, the strongest thing you can do
is stop trying to control how it unfolds.

Because real connection doesn't come from precision.
It comes from *trust.*

Trust doesn't mean faith in your partner's perfection.
It means faith in *the space between you.*
Faith that you can let go for a moment — and the

relationship won't collapse.
Faith that they can hold something without you managing
it.
Faith that you can survive an uncomfortable emotion
without steering it to safety.

Trust is terrifying for people who lead.
Because you're not used to letting others carry weight.
You believe responsibility equals control.
And the moment you let go, you fear it all falls apart.

But the truth is more confronting:

> *Control doesn't create stability.*
> *It creates tension.*
> *It creates hierarchy.*
> *It creates silent emotional suppression that*
> *looks like peace —*
> *but is actually just fear on mute.*

Letting go is not passive.
It's not abandoning the relationship.
It's *allowing* the relationship to breathe on its own —
without your hands around its neck.

It means trusting your partner's emotions
without reshaping them.
Trusting your own discomfort
without trying to escape it.
Trusting that closeness doesn't require perfection
— just presence.

The softest power is not the power to fix.
 It's the power to *stay open* when everything in you wants to shut down.
 It's the ability to say:
 "I don't know where this is going… but I'm not leaving."

No solutions.
 No schedule.
 No system.
 Just trust.

And in that space,
 something real can finally emerge.

You've mastered control.
 Now it's time to master *release.*

Not by giving up —
 but by giving space.

Because love doesn't grow under pressure.
 It grows in oxygen.

~~~~~

> *The most generous thing you can offer in love*
> *isn't protection, prediction, or planning.*
> *It's space.*
> *And the faith that what grows in that space*
> *will be stronger than anything you could've*
> *built alone.*

~~~~~

The ROI of Vulnerability

The Collapse That Connected Us

He didn't mean to cry.
 He didn't even think he could.
 Not after everything he'd been through.
 Not after years of performing strength so convincingly that
most people forgot to check if he was okay.

He was an athlete once. Now he runs a company.
 He leads with poise. People trust him.
 He's sharp, charismatic, in control.

But that night, at home,
 something cracked.

His wife said one thing — something ordinary — and
suddenly, he wasn't listening anymore.
 His chest got tight. His jaw clenched.
 And before he could stop himself, the words came out:

"I don't know what I'm doing."

He broke.

He cried in front of her for the first time in ten years.
 Not just a tear. A collapse.
 The dam he'd held up for a decade gave way —
 and all the shame, the pressure, the confusion, the fear…
it poured out.

He expected her to recoil.
 To lose respect.
 To retreat from the mess he'd kept so carefully hidden.

But she didn't flinch.
She didn't fix it.
She didn't shrink.

She moved closer.

Not because she liked seeing him in pain —
but because for the first time in their marriage,
he wasn't performing.
He was *present*.

And for the first time,
she felt like she was holding *him* —
not the version of him he built to be admired.

This is what most high performers never experience until
it's too late:

The collapse doesn't end the relationship.
It begins it.

The moment you finally stop curating yourself —
when you stop trying to appear "okay,"
when you say something real, even if it's ugly —
that's when intimacy shows up.

Because now,
there's no act between you.

Now they don't have to guess.
Now they don't have to chase you for truth.
Now they know what's underneath the competence.

And maybe for the first time,
you're not alone.

You think your partner wants you to be strong.

But what they actually want is to see your *humanity*
— and to be trusted with it.

Not because they can fix it.
But because your willingness to *bring it to them*
is what makes them feel close to you.

Without that?
They're loving a mask.
Sleeping beside a statue.
Reaching for someone who never really lets them in.

The collapse is not the end of your image.
It's the start of your relationship.

Because the moment you stop managing their perception
of you —
you give them access to the one thing they've wanted all
along:

The real you.

~~~~

What breaks you open
is often the very thing
that finally makes you feel held.

~~~~

Strength vs. Safety

You think you're being strong.

You keep your emotions contained.
 You stay calm in conflict.
 You don't burden your partner with what you're carrying.
 You lead with solutions.
 You never show weakness.

You call it love.
 They experience it as distance.

Because while you're trying to be *strong*,
 what your partner is looking for is something else entirely:

Safety.

And here's the truth you were never taught:
 Emotional strength is not the same as emotional safety.

Strength says, *"I've got this."*
 Safety says, *"You don't have to hold this alone."*

Strength controls the narrative.
 Safety opens the door.

Strength hides the mess to protect others.
 Safety says, *"This is where I'm really at — and I trust you to see it."*

You've been taught that being unshakable is love.
That stoicism is compassion.
That keeping it together is how you protect the people you care about.

But ask yourself this:
Have you ever actually *felt* close to someone who never lets you in?
Have you ever relaxed around someone whose mask never slips?

Neither has your partner.

Because no matter how composed you are,
if your partner never sees the full range of your emotions
—
they will never feel fully connected to you.

They will admire you.
They may even love you.
But they won't feel *safe*.

And without safety,
love becomes a performance — not a sanctuary.

This is the blind spot:

**You think your strength makes the relationship safer.
But it often makes your partner feel more alone.**

Because they're carrying not only their own emotions —
but all the ones you're hiding, too.

You've armored yourself to be dependable.
But in doing so, you've become impenetrable.

And nothing can grow in a space where nothing is allowed to move.

What your partner needs most is not your solution.
 Not your silence.
 Not your strength.

What they need is your *honesty*.
 Even if it's ugly.
 Even if it's unprocessed.
 Even if it doesn't make you look like the composed, high-functioning partner you try so hard to be.

Because your truth —
 raw, imperfect, vulnerable —
 is the only thing that makes you *real* to them.

~~~~~

Your strength makes you impressive.
Your openness makes you safe.

~~~~~

The Rock and the Power of Transparency

Dwayne Johnson — *The Rock* — built his empire on strength.

Physically. Commercially. Emotionally.

He's the kind of man people look at and think:
"That guy can handle anything."

And in many ways, he can.
 He's disciplined. Focused. Kind. Strategic.
 He works harder than most people dream of.
 He's turned performance into art, masculinity into myth,
and charisma into a business model.

But beneath the surface of all that power,
 something surprising happened:

He started telling the truth.

Over the last decade, Johnson began opening up —
 about depression.
 About moments of deep doubt.
 About feeling abandoned.
 About struggling in relationships.
 About emotional collapse.

He shared that he'd hit rock bottom more than once.
 And instead of losing admiration,
 people trusted him *more*.

Because transparency didn't make him less strong —
 it made him *human*.

And people don't fall in love with your strength.
 They fall in love with your *humanity*.

This is what most high performers miss:

**Your strength is not diminished by vulnerability.
It's revealed by it.**

When you share what hurts —
 not as a headline, not as a strategy, not as a story you've
already conquered —
 but as something *real*, still alive in your chest...

That's when people feel closest to you.
 That's when your partner leans in, instead of pulling away.

And that's when you stop being *admired* from a distance,
 and start being *loved* up close.

The Rock didn't lose his image by being transparent.
 He deepened it.
 He expanded it.

He showed that masculinity — and leadership — doesn't
mean emotional silence.
 It means emotional courage.

The courage to say:
 "I don't have it all figured out."
 "I've struggled, too."
 "I hurt, and I need support sometimes."

And it turns out, that's what makes people trust you.
 Not the armor.
 The *honesty beneath it.*

You can still be strong.
But strength without vulnerability is intimidation.
It's impressive — but it's not connective.

And if you're not willing to be seen in your tenderness,
you'll never be fully received in your love.

~~~~~

*You won't lose respect by telling the truth.
You'll finally start being loved for more than
your strength.*

~~~~~

Emotional Exposure as Investment

You understand risk.

You've made bold moves in business.
You've bet on uncertain outcomes.
You've sacrificed comfort for growth more times than you
can count.

You understand that *nothing real grows without exposure.*

But when it comes to love?
You hesitate.
You hedge.

You want guarantees.
You want the connection before the confession.

You want to be sure you won't lose something before you show something.

That's not investment.
That's *emotional risk aversion*.

And it's costing you the one thing you can't build without vulnerability:
intimacy.

Here's the paradox of love, for people like you:

**You've built your life on calculated risk.
But in your relationship, you only take emotional action when the return feels guaranteed.**

That's not how trust works.
That's not how closeness works.

In relationships, your vulnerability *is* the investment.
You go first.
You open.
You put something on the table that might not be met, fixed, or understood right away.

Not to manipulate the outcome —
but to invite something deeper than performance.

Because *without risk, there is no return.*

Think about the people you trust most in life.

Is it because they're perfect?
Is it because they never cracked?

Or is it because you saw them tell the truth when it was
inconvenient?
Because you watched them own their fear, their shame,
their mess —
and stay standing?

That's the moment trust deepens:
when someone shows you what *costs* them to reveal.

And that's what your partner is waiting for, too.

Not your next insight.
Not your next strategy for listening better.
But your *emotional exposure*.   .
Your realness.

Every relationship grows or dies
based on one thing:
**how much risk you're willing to take
without knowing what you'll get back.**

That's not weakness.
That's the emotional version of courage.

And if you're brave enough to lead in boardrooms,
you're brave enough to lead in your living room, too.

Not with structure.
But with sincerity.

Not with the perfect words.
But with the *real* ones.

~~~~~

Vulnerability is the highest-leverage move in love.
It requires no perfection.
Just your willingness to go first —
and stay open, even when you can't see the return yet.

~~~~~

Take Off the Armor

You wear it so well,
 you probably forgot you put it on.

The steady tone.
 The calm delivery.
 The intellectual precision.
 The endless competence.

You think this is who you are.

But it's not.

It's who you learned to be
 to stay respected.
 To stay safe.
 To stay in control.

That's your armor.

And at some point, it stopped protecting you
and started *isolating* you.

You thought it made you strong.
But it's kept you from connection.

Because your partner doesn't want the curated version of
you.
They don't want the "always okay" version.
They don't want your best self if it means they never get to
hold your *whole* self.

They want the moments you've been taught to hide.
The ones where you tremble.
Where you don't have the answer.
Where you ask for reassurance and mean it.

Where you drop the image and say:
"This is me. I hope you'll stay."

That's the moment they get to love you —
not the version of you they were supposed to admire,
but the version of you they can actually *touch*.

You don't have to collapse to connect.
You don't need to bleed every emotion you've ever
hidden.
You just have to stop *pretending you don't need to be
seen.*

Because no one can love you
if you keep insisting you're fine.

Take off the armor.

Not all at once.
 Not recklessly.
 Just enough to feel the breeze hit your skin again.

Just enough to say:
 *"I'm not here to impress you anymore.
 I'm here to be known."*

Because that's what real love is.
 Not performance.
 Not protection.

Revelation.

~~~~~

> *You put the armor on to survive.
> But you'll have to take it off to be loved.*

~~~~~

The Fear of Being Known

The Charming Disguise

He's warm.
He's attentive.
He never raises his voice, never forgets a birthday, never walks away from a tough conversation.

He's a great partner — everyone says so.
Friends adore him. His team respects him. Even his exes say he's a "good man."

But the person sleeping beside him feels like they're talking to a beautifully programmed version of love.
Not a person.
A performance.

Because whenever they get close to something raw, something real —
he shifts.
Cracks a joke.
Compliments her.
Asks a thoughtful question that gently moves the moment away from him.

And slowly, she starts to disappear in the relationship.
Not because he doesn't care.
But because he never actually *shows up*.

This is what emotional evasion looks like at the highest level:
Charm as a defense mechanism.

It's not malicious.
It's not dishonest.
It's a skill — built over years of learning how to be likable,
emotionally fluent, and hard to criticize.

You can talk about your past.
You can name your patterns.
You can explain your triggers.
But you never actually *let someone in while you're feeling
them.*

You stay half a step ahead of real vulnerability —
always available, never exposed.

You think you're being open.
But you're being *curated.*
Polished. Controlled.

Your partner doesn't feel close to you.
They feel managed by you.

Because behind the generosity… is distance.
Behind the warmth… is avoidance.
Behind the emotional intelligence… is a person who is
terrified of being truly *seen.*

This is the charming disguise:
You're so good at love that you never actually risk it.
You know what to say.
You know how to show up.
You know how to be admired.

But admiration is not intimacy.
And performance is not presence.

You keep giving people reasons to love you —
while refusing to give them *access* to who you are when you're not performing.

And that's how you become deeply loved —
but never truly known.

~~~~~

Charm makes you lovable.
Vulnerability makes you real.
And love without realness is just applause in disguise.

~~~~~

The Cost of the Mask

You've become excellent at being "yourself."

Polished. Articulate. Thoughtful.
Just vulnerable enough to seem real,
but never messy enough to feel out of control.

You know how to talk about your emotions
without ever actually *being in them*.
You know how to reflect on your childhood, your patterns, your mistakes
— but from a safe emotional distance.

You're not hiding.
You're *curating*.

And the people around you can feel it.
Especially the person who loves you.

At first, your partner is impressed.

They've never been with someone so self-aware,
so communicative, so emotionally competent.

But after a while, they start to feel... alone.

Because you never bring them your uncertainty in real
time.
You never let them see what's *underneath* the insight.
You never show them the parts of you that don't have a
script yet.

You're always composed.
Always available.
Always a few feet back from whatever's actually alive in
the moment.

They don't feel your chaos.
Your ache.
Your need.

And without that, they start to wonder:

> If I've never seen the unguarded version of
> you...
> have I ever really seen you at all?

This is the cost of the mask:
**It protects you from being rejected for who you are —
but it also guarantees you'll never be loved for who
you are.**

Because the more convincing your persona,
 the more disconnected your partner feels from your *inner
world*.

Not because they don't love you —
 but because you won't let them in.

You're still trying to be impressive
 in a space that only gets real when you *stop performing*.

If you want closeness,
 you have to stop editing in real time.
 You have to let the sentence come out wrong.
 You have to admit you don't know.
 You have to let your partner meet the parts of you
 that don't match the image you've spent your life
perfecting.

Because if your partner never sees your mess,
 they're not in love with *you*.
 They're in love with your control.

And that's not intimacy.
 That's theater.

~~~~~

If you're always being understood but never
being felt,
 you're not connecting —
 you're performing safety for someone who's
starving for your truth.

~~~~~

Robin Williams and the Vanishing Act

Robin Williams was unforgettable.

He lit up every room.
 Exploded on every screen.
 His speed of thought, his physicality, his voice, his soul —
it all felt infinite.

He didn't just perform. He *became.*
 Whatever the moment needed — laughter, comfort,
genius, tenderness — he gave it.

And yet, behind all that brilliance,
 he was disappearing.

Not in front of an audience.
 In private.
 With the people who wanted to *know* him — not just
receive him.

In interviews, friends and loved ones described a man who
was always "on."
 Not because he was faking — but because silence
terrified him.
 Stillness made him vulnerable.

Being known meant being exposed — and he wasn't sure what people would do with that version of him.

So he gave them brilliance instead.

Charm. Warmth. Genius.
And the world adored him.

But that adoration didn't save him.
Because **being admired by everyone
is not the same as being truly known by someone.**

This is the vanishing act.

You become so good at meeting everyone else's needs,
 you forget how to let anyone meet yours.

You use humor, generosity, caretaking — even emotional intelligence —
 to deflect from your own vulnerability.

You become beloved.
 And profoundly alone.

Because no one sees you.
 Not really.

They see the light you emit —
 but never the person holding the match.

You don't have to be a celebrity to live this.
 You just have to be someone

who's mastered connection as a skill
and forgotten how to let it be a feeling.

You can give love to everyone around you
without ever letting it land on *you.*

And when that happens,
your partner begins to feel like they're loving someone
through glass.
Close, visible, almost reachable —
but never quite touchable.

This section isn't about Robin.
It's about you.

The part of you that believes
if you can stay entertaining, generous, helpful, or "good,"
then you'll be safe.
Then you'll be loved.

But love doesn't want the performance.
It wants the *person behind it.*

And you'll never feel truly loved
until you're brave enough to show someone
the version of you that doesn't need to win them over.

~~~~~

If you keep giving people your light
but never let them hold your shadow,
you'll always be adored —
but never truly known.

~~~~~

Why Being Seen Feels So Dangerous

You don't hide because you're manipulative.
 You hide because, at some point,
 being fully seen didn't feel safe.

Maybe you learned that love had conditions.
 That being "a lot" made people pull away.
 That being too emotional, too intense, too unpredictable
got you punished — or ignored.

So you adapted.

You became likable.
 Capable.
 Resilient.
 You got good at managing how others experienced you.

And somewhere along the way,
 you began to equate emotional exposure with emotional
danger.

That fear never left — it just got dressed in success.

Now, instead of asking for what you need,
 you become the person no one has to worry about.

Instead of telling your partner you're struggling,
 you double down on being supportive.

Instead of showing your contradictions,
 you stay consistent — even when you're breaking inside.

You've built an identity around being easy to love.
 And now the thought of being loved *without* that image?

Terrifying.

Because if they see the version of you that's still insecure,
uncertain, messy...
 what if they walk?

What if the love you've earned
 only works as long as you don't change?

This is why being seen feels so dangerous:
 it removes your control over the outcome.

When you're performing, you get to shape the story.
 When you're honest, you're at the mercy of someone
else's reaction.

And for someone used to being five steps ahead —
 that's unbearable.

So you stay in the performance.
 Not because it's glamorous.
 But because it's safer.

You think you're protecting yourself.
 But what you're actually doing
 is blocking the one thing you're craving most:
 to be loved without conditions.

You don't need to be perfect to be loved.
 You need to be *reachable*.
 You need to be *willing*
 to let someone see the parts of you that haven't been
optimized yet.

Because love that only touches your image
never reaches your heart.

~~~~~

*Being loved for who you show the world is
comforting.*
*Being loved for who you really are is terrifying
— and necessary.*

~~~~~

The Bravery of Letting Someone In

You've done brave things.

You've launched ideas no one believed in.
You've made impossible decisions.
You've risked failure, rejection, humiliation — and kept
going.

But here's the one thing you still haven't done:

Let someone all the way in.
Not into your story.
Not into your curated past.
Not into the version of you that performs intimacy
perfectly.

But into the moment where you say,
"I don't know how to be fully loved, and I'm trying anyway."

That's real courage.
That's what love is asking for.

You don't have to fall apart.
You don't have to bare your soul in a grand confession.

You just have to stop editing yourself
when things get emotionally close.

You just have to stop reaching for control
the moment someone steps toward your truth.

You just have to stay *a few seconds longer*
when the conversation starts to feel unfamiliar —
and trust that you won't disappear if someone sees what
you usually hide.

Letting someone in isn't one big act.
It's a thousand small decisions:

- Letting your partner see you when you don't have answers.

- Admitting you're hurt instead of acting like you're above it.

- Saying "I need you right now" without flinching.

- Telling the truth when it's inconvenient, awkward, or incomplete.

- Staying present when you feel the impulse to perform.

That's what it looks like.
Not polished.
Not poetic.
Just honest.
And brave as hell.

You want to be loved for who you really are?
Then you have to risk showing them.

That's it.

No one can connect with what you never reveal.
And no one can love the self you keep behind glass.

~~~~

At some point, you have to decide:
You can keep being admired.
Or you can be fully known.
But not both at the same time.

~~~~

High Standards, Low Safety

The Silent Retreat

She didn't yell.
 She didn't criticize.
 She didn't belittle him in front of others.

She just held the bar.

High.

She planned the vacations.
 Scheduled the cleaners.
 Ran the house.
 Handled the finances.
 Crushed it at work.

And when he tried to help —
 he did it wrong.

He booked the wrong hotel.
 Forgot the birthday gift.
 Said the wrong thing during dinner.
 Didn't read the room.
 Didn't listen fast enough.
 Didn't move fast enough.

And slowly… he stopped trying.

Not out of resentment.
 Not out of spite.

Out of *exhaustion*.

Because being in a relationship with someone who
expects excellence in everything —
including how you love them —
isn't inspiring.
It's *crushing*.

He didn't feel loved.
He felt managed.

Like he was being watched, evaluated, adjusted.

Even her compliments had a tone:
"Thanks for finally doing it that way."
"See how much easier it is when you listen?"

So he stopped leaning in.
Not because he didn't care.
But because he *never felt like he could get it right anyway.*

This is how emotional retreat happens in high-pressure
relationships:
not with explosions — but with quiet exits.
The partner doesn't rebel.
They disappear.

They stop bringing new ideas.
They stop initiating.
They start second-guessing everything before they say it.

Not because they lack strength —
but because the environment trained them to shrink.

You may not mean to create this climate.
You may think you're just being clear.
Helpful. Mature.

But clarity without softness becomes critique.
Structure without warmth becomes performance.
And high standards without emotional safety become
emotional *conditions*.

It sounds like:

- *"I just want you to try harder."*

- *"I need you to be more aware."*

- *"I can't always be the one holding it together."*

All valid.
All fair.

But if your partner only feels love when they're doing it
right,
they'll eventually stop reaching for it at all.

Because love that's only available on your terms
never feels like love.
It feels like an exam.

~~~~~

Sometimes your partner didn't give up.
They just got tired of being graded.

~~~~~

Perfectionism as Protection

You think you're being responsible.

You set high standards — for yourself, for your partner, for the relationship.
 You don't ask for anything you wouldn't give.
 You want clarity. Accountability. Growth.

You're not trying to be difficult.
 You're trying to build something that *works*.

But underneath that structure is something much older.
 Much softer.
 Much more afraid.

You're not just demanding excellence.
 You're protecting yourself —
 from chaos, from disappointment, from pain.

And your perfectionism isn't just about doing things right.
 It's about staying *safe* in a world that often made you feel unsafe when things got messy.

Here's how it starts:

Maybe as a child, you learned that being good meant being loved.
 That order meant peace.
 That emotions were tolerated only when they were clean, reasoned, controlled.

So you became excellent.

You built routines. Systems. Expectations.
You stayed three steps ahead of discomfort.
You managed your world so well
that no one ever had to see how scared you were
underneath.

And now in love —
you're still doing it.

Perfectionism is not cruelty.
It's fear in a leadership role.

It says:

- "I don't want to be hurt by your inconsistency."

- "I don't want to be caught off guard by your failure."

- "I don't want to need you and not be met."

So instead of asking directly for reassurance, for softness,
for support,
you *raise the bar*.

You ask for "better communication,"
when what you really want is emotional closeness.
You point out the mistake,
when what you really need is presence.
You critique how they show love,
because you're terrified they'll stop trying altogether.

You're not wrong for wanting quality.
 But here's the truth:

**The more pressure you apply to your partner's performance,
 the less emotionally honest they'll become.**

They'll start managing your reactions instead of expressing their reality.
 They'll second-guess their instincts.
 They'll under-function — not because they're lazy, but because they're scared.

Not of *you*.
 But of the space between you — and how conditional it feels.

This is the hidden danger of perfectionism in love:

It creates precision.
 But it eliminates intimacy.

Because love is not about getting it right.
 It's about staying in it when it *goes wrong* — and making your partner feel safe in the process.

And safety doesn't come from being corrected.
 It comes from being *received*.

~~~~

Perfectionism doesn't create connection.
It creates compliance.

*And if your partner feels like they can never
be enough —
eventually, they'll stop trying to be.*

~~~~~

Anna Wintour and the Freeze of Elegance

Anna Wintour is a force.

She redefined an industry.
 Set the pace for global fashion.
 Made precision into power.

People describe her presence as electric.
 Elegant. Unshakeable.
 Her silence is louder than most people's voices.

She's not cruel.
 She's just *clear*.
 Clear in vision. Clear in taste. Clear in standards.

And that clarity created legacy.

But it also created something else —
 a quiet emotional freeze around her.

In memoirs, interviews, and portrayals from those who've
worked with her,
 a pattern emerges:

She's brilliant.
 And emotionally unavailable.

She's calm under pressure —
but distant under vulnerability.

She demands excellence —
but rarely offers warmth.

People show up for her.
But they rarely feel *held* by her.

And while she is respected, admired, feared, and followed
—
she is not often described as someone people feel safe
around.

This is not a takedown of Anna Wintour.
It's a mirror for those of us who lead with control,
elegance, and impossibly high expectations.

Because it shows us the truth:
**your standard can command the room —
and still chill the people closest to you.**

When you're that clear,
people stop offering you their rawness.
They bring you only what's polished, rehearsed, and pre-
approved.

They show you what they think you want to see —
because showing you anything else
feels like taking an emotional risk you didn't sign up for.

And over time,
 your relationship becomes full of refinement,
 but empty of *aliveness*.

Because no one feels safe falling apart
 in front of someone who never lets themselves unravel.

Elegance isn't the enemy.
 Leadership isn't the problem.
 Clarity is not cold.

But when your partner is always trying not to disappoint
you —
 you're no longer in a relationship.
 You're in a performance loop.

And love, by nature, is *imperfect*.

It breathes.
 It trembles.
 It contradicts itself.
 It evolves in conversation, not commands.

And if you want real intimacy,
 you have to trade a little control
 for a lot more truth.

~~~~~

Your presence may command the world —
 but if no one feels emotionally free around
 you,

you're not leading a relationship.
You're freezing it.

~~~~~

When Love Feels Like a Performance Review

It's not what you say.
It's how it feels.

You think you're just asking for what you need.
Setting expectations.
Calling in more effort.
Trying to "build something better together."

But your partner hears something else entirely:
"You're not enough."
"You keep messing up."
"You'll be loved… when you get it right."

And slowly, being with you starts to feel like a performance review.

Not a relationship.

They start monitoring themselves.
Double-checking every word.
Playing conversations back in their head before they even speak.

Not because you're harsh —
but because you're exacting.

Not because you're demanding —
but because they can feel your disappointment before you
say a word.

They know the look.
The pause.
The correction.
The "we need to talk."

And over time, their nervous system learns:
This isn't where I go to be vulnerable.
This is where I go to be evaluated.

You don't mean to make them feel this way.
You're not cruel.
You're not even unkind.

You're just tired of carrying the emotional weight alone.
You want more support.
You want initiative.
You want someone who shows up the way *you* show up.

But here's the thing:
**If love only feels available when they're performing
correctly,**
it stops feeling like love.

It starts feeling like a job.
With KPIs.
And consequences.

And no one feels free when they're being graded.

Eventually, they'll stop being honest with you.
Not because they're hiding something —
but because they can't afford the feedback loop anymore.

They'll say what they think you want to hear.
They'll do just enough to avoid "the talk."
They'll shrink the parts of themselves that frustrate you
until you're living with a version of them that is technically
functional —
and emotionally gone.

And you'll wonder why they've changed.

They didn't.
They just got tired of losing points.

This is what happens when high standards override
emotional safety:
You get compliance instead of connection.
Obedience instead of presence.
Partnership that performs —
but doesn't breathe.

~~~~~

If your partner feels like they have to earn your
love every day,
they'll eventually stop believing they're worthy
of it at all.

~~~~~

Creating Safety Without Lowering the Bar

You don't need to settle.
 You don't need to abandon your vision.
 You don't need to become "easier" just to be loved.

But you do need to ask yourself one question:

**Is my standard creating intimacy —
 or compliance?**

Because high standards are not the problem.
 Conditional love is.

Your relationship shouldn't be built on who gets it "right."
 It should be built on who's *safe to grow with.*

There's a difference between leadership and pressure.
 Between raising the bar and pulling someone out of
themselves to meet it.
 Between inspiring your partner and exhausting them with
your expectations.

Your partner doesn't need you to lower your standards.
 They need to know they can be in process —
without being penalized.

That if they mess up, they'll be met with curiosity, not
critique.
 That if they fall short, the connection won't vanish.
 That if they bring you something raw, unpolished, or
imperfect —
 you won't pull away.

That's not leniency.
That's **emotional safety**.
And safety is what allows people to rise.

You don't get the best out of someone by making love conditional.
You get the best out of them by making love *available*, even when they're not at their best.

Not unaccountable.
But unpunished.

Because no one grows inside a relationship
where every moment feels like a test.

People evolve when they feel *invited*,
not evaluated.

So keep your clarity.
Keep your strength.
Keep your brilliance.

But soften the space between you.
Make room for fumbles.
Make space for difference.
Make safety a higher standard than perfection.

Because love isn't what happens when everything is done right.
Love is what makes it safe to try again,
when it's gone wrong.

~~~~~

You don't have to lower the bar.
You just have to stop holding it like a weapon.
Because no one thrives under pressure
when the thing they're afraid of losing is you.

~~~~~

From Strategy to Surrender

The Calendar of Intimacy

He thought he was doing everything right.

Weekly date night.
 Biweekly check-ins.
 A shared Google doc titled *"Connection Goals."*

He read the books.
 Listened to the podcasts.
 Even got them into couples therapy — *before* there was a major problem.

He wasn't avoiding the relationship.
 He was optimizing it.

But one night, over dinner, his partner said it:

"I don't want to be another item on your agenda."

She wasn't angry.
 Just tired.
 Tired of being *managed*.
 Tired of being *included*, but never *felt*.

Because all the rituals, all the structure, all the systems —
 still left her emotionally alone.

This is what high performers often miss:
 Structure isn't surrender.
 Presence isn't planning.
 And intimacy doesn't live in your calendar.

You can build all the right systems
and still be unreachable.

Because no amount of scheduling creates emotional
openness.
No check-in ritual guarantees depth.
No "intimacy night" means anything
if you're still performing your part rather than *living the
moment.*

He was showing up.
He was invested.
But he was still in charge.

He never let love lead.

He tried to guide the relationship like a project —
and forgot that relationships aren't built on guidance.
They're built on *giving yourself over to something
unknown.*

And love can feel that.
Your partner can feel that.

They know when the room is full of presence —
and when it's just full of effort.

The truth is:
You can't control your way into closeness.
You can't engineer your way into intimacy.
You can't "optimize" your way into feeling alive with
someone.

At some point,
 you have to stop trying to manage the relationship
 and start *being inside it.*

No agenda.
 No plan.
 No point system.

Just:
 "I'm here.
 I don't know what this moment will bring.
 But I'm not leaving it early."

~~~~

Connection isn't something you schedule.
 It's something you surrender to.

~~~~

When Presence Replaces Planning

At first, your plans made you feel responsible.
 Mature. Intentional.

You set reminders to "check in emotionally."
 You blocked off time for deep connection.
 You scheduled "us" — like everything else that matters in
your life.

It wasn't performative.
 It was sincere.

But here's the thing:
You were still in control.

Still curating the terms.
 Still determining when and how love would be allowed to show up.
 Still bracing, managing, timing it all.

And love could feel that.

Because the one thing love won't do
 is perform on command.

Love doesn't need your plan.
 It needs your presence.

And presence isn't just a time slot.
 It's your full nervous system saying:
 "I'm here. Not managing. Not correcting. Not preparing for what's next. Just here."

That's what your partner has been asking for all along.
 Not your structure.
 Not your systems.
 Not your emotional intelligence.

Your attention.
 Unarmored.
 Unstructured.
 Uninterrupted.

Here's the shift:

Presence isn't about "holding space."
It's about *entering* the space.
With your full body.
With no script.
With nothing to fix, and nothing to prove.

Because connection doesn't happen when everything is prepared.
It happens when you let the moment surprise you.

You think showing up means planning for the moment.
But it actually means *responding* to the moment.
Letting it move you.
Letting it change you.
Letting it be real — even if it's messy or off-script.

And your partner knows the difference.

They know when you're doing closeness
versus *being in it*.

They know when you're saying the right words
but holding tension in your chest.

They know when you're managing the moment
instead of *living it with them*.

You don't need more planning.
You need more pauses.
More silence.
More "I don't know what to say right now, but I'm not leaving."

Because that's what presence actually is:
**The willingness to let love be unscheduled,
unpredictable,
and completely alive.**

~~~~~

*Planning keeps you in control.
Presence sets you free.*

~~~~~

Ray Dalio and Radical Relational Openness

Ray Dalio built a billion-dollar empire on principles.
He made transparency a business model.
He championed radical honesty, real-time feedback, and
clear emotional protocol.

In his world, there are rules for how to be truthful.
Guidelines for conflict.
Standards for openness.

It's brilliant.
And in many ways, it works.

But even Dalio admits:
radical transparency doesn't always feel good.
It can be awkward.
Raw.
Uncomfortable.

Because no matter how you structure it,
**real connection doesn't come from saying the right
things —**

135

it comes from staying in the discomfort long enough to become real.

You can adopt all the systems.
Clear the air weekly.
Create rituals of communication.

And still miss each other entirely
if your vulnerability is only allowed inside a framework.

Because life doesn't ask for "principled responses."
It asks for *emotional presence.*

Your partner doesn't want a conflict-resolution matrix.
They want to know you're here when the moment gets hot
—

not just that you'll "circle back with clarity."

They want you to tremble, stay, and speak from the *middle*
of something.
Not the post-analysis.
Not the planned debrief.
Not the memo.

Dalio's brilliance shows us something crucial:
structure can create the *conditions* for emotional truth
—

but it cannot *replace* emotional surrender.

And surrender isn't a process.
It's a choice.

A moment where you stop explaining your truth
and start *feeling* it, in real time, with someone else.

It's the difference between saying "I'm hurt"
and *letting them see it in your eyes before the words are ready.*

It's the difference between a system
and a soul.

You don't build intimacy by optimizing how you express.
You build it by becoming someone
who doesn't need to be perfect when the truth arrives.

And sometimes the most radical thing you can do
is shut the systems down
and let the silence fill the room —
until something real comes out that neither of you
expected.

~~~~~

*Transparency without vulnerability is just a
data dump.*
Real intimacy begins when the plan ends.

~~~~~

Why Strategy Stops Working

Strategy got you here.

It built your career.
Helped you navigate complexity.

Kept you calm when others unraveled.
It gave you an edge in every room you entered.

It made you effective.
Respected.
Unshakable.

So when the relationship felt off, you did what you always do:
You created a plan.

Better questions.
Better routines.
Better delivery.
Better execution.

But nothing changed.
Or if it did — it didn't *feel* different.

Because strategy doesn't create intimacy.
It creates outcomes.

And intimacy isn't an outcome.
It's an *unfolding*.

This is the moment high performers quietly break down:

When they've done everything right —
they've improved, they've adapted, they've learned —
and their partner still says:
"I don't feel close to you."

And suddenly, none of it computes.

Because they were solving for love.
But love doesn't need a solver.
It needs a *witness*.
A participant.
A real, emotionally exposed human being who isn't trying to manage the moment —
but to *feel it.*

Here's why strategy fails:
It's still about control.

Strategy says:

- "If I do this, I'll get that."

- "If I stay calm, they'll feel safe."

- "If I improve communication, they'll soften."

- "If I give them what they want, they'll give me what I need."

But love doesn't run on inputs and outputs.
Love doesn't respond to precision.
It responds to *presence*.
It expands with surrender.

And no matter how sophisticated your system is,
if it's still about getting the moment *right*,
you're still not in it.

This doesn't mean give up.
It means *let go.*

Let go of the need to win.
To control the outcome.
To manage their perception of you.

Because the moment you stop *guiding* the relationship
and start *feeling* it — raw, unrehearsed, imperfect —
is the moment it becomes real.

~~~~~

The more you try to perfect love,
the more it escapes you.
Because love doesn't need you to solve it —
it needs you to surrender to it.

~~~~~

Practicing the Let-Go

Letting go doesn't mean checking out.
It doesn't mean you stop caring.
It doesn't mean you stop showing up.

Letting go means this:
You stop gripping the moment
as if it owes you an outcome.

You stop turning love into a strategy.
You stop trying to get it right.
You stop using self-improvement as a shield from
emotional risk.

Instead, you say:
"This is where I am.
This is what I feel.
And I'm willing to stay in it — even if it's messy."

That's surrender.
Not silence.
Not apathy.
Honest presence without a plan.

You want to love better?

Let your partner see the part of you that doesn't have it all figured out.
Not for drama. Not for attention.
Just for *truth*.

Let the moment unfold before you manage it.
Speak before you perfect the words.
Feel before you fix.

Sit in the silence that makes your stomach twist.
Let the discomfort *stay* long enough to show you what's underneath it.

Because that's where love actually lives —
in the part of the experience you keep trying to organize.

This is the practice:

- When you feel the urge to analyze, breathe instead.

- When you want to teach, ask a question instead.

- When you want to rescue, hold their hand instead.

- When you want to explain, just say, *"I hear you. I'm here."*

You'll be shocked what happens
when you stop *guiding* your partner
and start *meeting* them.

You don't need to lose your discipline.
You just need to remember that love doesn't thrive on control.
It thrives on your willingness to *be changed* by the moment.

That's the let-go.

Not giving up —
but giving *in*
to what connection wants to become,
without trying to steer it every step of the way.

~~~~~

You don't fall in love with someone's strategy.
You fall in love with their surrender.
And they fall for you
when you finally stop managing —
and start being real.

~~~~~

Listening Like a Leader

The Interruption Reflex

He didn't cut her off mid-sentence.
He waited until she was done.

He nodded.
Maintained eye contact.
Did everything a "good communicator" is supposed to do.

But halfway through her sharing something vulnerable,
she stopped. Looked at him.
And said:

"I can feel you already thinking about your answer."

That was the moment it hit him.
He wasn't listening.
He was **preparing.**

High performers are taught to lead conversations, not
follow them.
To track information, anticipate outcomes, shape
responses.
You pride yourself on efficiency. Clarity. Insight.

But love isn't looking for insight.
It's looking for *intimacy.*

And intimacy doesn't happen when you're calculating your
next move.
It happens when you stop trying to move at all.

This is the interruption reflex:
You don't always interrupt with words.
You interrupt with *energy*.
With the hum of your brain preparing a counterpoint.
With the tension in your body as you wait for the "real issue" to reveal itself.
With the subtle shift that says,
"I'm almost ready to fix this."

And your partner can feel it.

They feel you speeding ahead.
They feel the gap between what they're saying
and what you're already organizing into meaning.

They feel your restraint — not your *reception.*

You think listening is about timing.
It's not.
It's about stillness.

Not external.
Internal.

It's about staying where they are —
not rushing ahead to where you *think* the moment is going.

Because even if you wait for them to finish,
if your attention is already gone,
your silence isn't presence —
it's *performance.*

Real listening doesn't begin with your ears.
It begins with your willingness to *slow down your need to respond.*

To stop solving.
Stop shaping.
Stop holding space only to fill it with your insight.

Instead —
let the moment be theirs.
Let their words hang in the air without chasing them down.
Let the pause after their sentence be a space of trust —
not tension.

Let them feel that you're not here to fix the moment.
You're here to feel it *with* them.

~~~~~

*If you're already preparing your reply,
you've already left the conversation.*

~~~~~

How Fixing Disguises Itself as Listening

You think you're listening.

You're attentive.
You're patient.
You don't interrupt.

But underneath the surface, something else is happening:
You're scanning for the problem.

You're tracking tone.
 Flagging inconsistencies.
 Mapping her words onto a mental whiteboard labeled
"Solution."

And the moment she pauses,
 you deliver your insight.
 Kindly. Calmly.
 Maybe even brilliantly.

But she doesn't soften.

She looks disappointed.
 Or colder.
 Or suddenly tired.

And you're confused — because you were *trying*.

What just happened?

Here's what happened:
She didn't feel heard.
She felt *handled*.

You weren't listening.
 You were *fixing*.
 Disguised as empathy.
 Disguised as presence.
 Disguised as love.

Fixing feels like care to the fixer.
 It feels like control to the person being fixed.

Because underneath your response is a subtle message:
"Your experience is something to resolve."
"Your feeling is inefficient."
"Let's move this along to a better version of itself."

That's not love.
That's optimization.

And optimization makes people feel *managed*, not met.

True listening doesn't improve the moment.
It *deepens* it.

It doesn't move things forward.
It slows things *down*.

It doesn't fix what's broken.
It *witnesses what's real*.

Here's the truth:

- If your partner feels "smoothed out" after talking to you, but not seen — you were fixing.

- If they feel like they've been redirected, but not received — you were fixing.

- If your silence was just a bridge to your next point — you weren't listening. You were preparing your pitch.

You don't need better insights.
You need better stillness.

A space inside you that says:
*"This doesn't need to become anything right now.
It just needs to be heard."*

Because when someone shares something vulnerable with you,
they're not asking for answers.
They're asking:
*"Can I give you this piece of me
without being changed by it?"*

And if you can hold that —
without adding, fixing, reframing, or nudging —
that's where trust is built.

~~~~~

*Fixing is what you do when you're too
uncomfortable to receive someone fully.
Listening is what you do when you're brave
enough not to.*

~~~~~

Barack Obama and the Art of the Long Pause

Barack Obama is known for his calm.

He listens carefully.
Responds deliberately.

Pauses just long enough to make you feel like he's considering something real.
Not just responding — *reflecting.*

It's one of the reasons people trust him.
He gives the moment gravity.

But behind that public grace, there was a more private lesson unfolding.

In her memoir *Becoming*, Michelle Obama writes candidly about their early years:
how even Barack — thoughtful, grounded, deeply intelligent —
had to *learn how to listen in marriage.*

He wasn't unkind.
He wasn't inattentive.

He just hadn't learned the difference between hearing her words
and *letting them land.*

Public listening is about timing.
Private listening is about surrender.

In public, a pause is a tool — to clarify, to persuade, to lead.

In love, a pause is a *gesture of trust.*
It says:
"What you said matters more than how I want to respond."

It's not for effect.
It's for *reverence.*

Many high performers are excellent public listeners.
 They reflect. They summarize. They validate.

But in private?
 They rush.

Not because they don't care —
 but because care, for them, often looks like *getting to the solution quickly.*

And their partner feels that.
 They feel the subtle pressure to be clear. To be brief. To be right.

They feel that the moment isn't allowed to expand.

So they begin to contract.

Barack had to slow down.
 Not as a leader — but as a husband.
 Not to prepare better arguments — but to *open to emotional presence.*

And it made all the difference.

Because even someone who commands a room
 must learn how to *share a moment.*

Not by guiding it.
 By *entering it fully.*

This is the invitation:

Let the long pause return.
 Not for drama.
 Not for control.
 But for *depth.*

Let their words echo inside you before you reach for a reply.
 Let their tone shape your nervous system before your mind races ahead.

Because the pause isn't empty.
 It's full of *connection waiting to be felt.*

~~~~~

The best listeners don't rush to respond.
They let silence become a form of love.

~~~~~

Listening Without a Script

You think you're doing it right.

You're nodding.
 You're holding eye contact.
 You're letting them finish.
 You're even reflecting back what they said.

You're "an amazing communicator."
 That's what people always tell you.

But your partner still feels far away.
Still guarded.
Still not fully *in it* with you.

Because even though you're doing everything *right*,
they can sense the truth:

You're not actually letting them touch you.

This is the difference between *hearing* and *receiving*.
Between tracking what someone says
and *letting it change you* in real time.

When you listen with a script —
even a good one —
you're still in control.
Still ahead of the moment.
Still performing "good listening" instead of *being moved.*

And love doesn't want your performance.
It wants your *contact.*

Here's what performance-listening sounds like:

- "So what I'm hearing is…"

- "I get it, but here's what's also true…"

- "Let's talk about how we can fix this."

- "I totally understand — I used to feel the same
  way."

154

All of these are *technically* supportive.
But they serve *you*.
They regulate your discomfort.
They give you something to *do*.

What your partner really needs
is for you to *stop doing*.

To sit in the space where nothing makes sense yet —
and choose to stay open anyway.

Real listening doesn't polish the moment.
It lets the moment *change the listener*.

That's the whole point.

If you walk away with nothing rearranged inside you,
you weren't listening.
You were collecting data.

If you're just waiting for your turn to reflect,
you're not connected — you're *positioning*.

If you're already organizing their emotion before it even
lands,
you're not making space — you're *trimming the edges*.

To listen without a script is to *risk feeling something new.*

To be altered.
Moved.
Disoriented.
To put down your polished response and say:

"I didn't expect that.
Let me sit with it."

And that,
 more than any perfect reply,
 is what tells someone:
 "You matter. Enough to slow me down."

~~~~~

 The best listeners don't impress.
 They absorb.
 And in doing so, they let love reshape them.

~~~~~

Let Them Land

Most people don't need you to say the perfect thing.
 They just need to know they *landed*.

That their words didn't disappear into polite nods or well-timed affirmations.
 That their truth didn't bounce off your strategy.
 That they didn't have to fight for space.

They need to feel like they made contact.

Not with your ears.
 With *you*.

When someone shares something vulnerable,
 they are extending a part of themselves across a divide.

156

A part that has no armor.
No polish.
No performance.

And in that moment, they're not asking for your wisdom.
They're asking:

*"Can I hand you this piece of me
without being redirected, refined, or reshaped?"*

That's what it means to let someone land.

To make enough space — internally and relationally —
for their emotion to arrive without resistance.

But most high performers can't sit still that long.
They interrupt the landing with insight.
With reassurance.
With frameworks.
With that little tilt of the head that says, *"I already know
where this is going."*

And suddenly the other person retreats.
Not because they weren't heard —
but because they didn't *arrive.*

To let someone land is to *slow yourself down enough*
that their words become more important than your next
move.

It means pausing after they finish speaking.
Not rushing to fill the silence.

Letting the moment echo.
Letting it *move you* before you move it.

Because when someone feels they've landed,
 something in them *relaxes.*

The self-protection falls away.
 The tone softens.
 The conversation deepens — not because it was productive,
 but because it was *safe.*

Letting someone land doesn't mean you have no response.
 It means your response *starts with reverence.*

You receive first.
 You speak second.
 You let their words take up space before you try to shape the room again.

That's what makes people trust you.
 Not that you get it right.
 But that you let their truth stay whole when it gets to you.

~~~~

The deepest intimacy begins
not with what you say —
but with how fully you let them arrive.

~~~~

How to Fail Better Together

The Couple Who Didn't Break

It should have ended them.

The affair wasn't long.
 There wasn't a secret second life.
 Just one moment —
 one crossing of a line
 that broke something sacred between them.

She found out.
 He confessed.
 They collapsed.

But they didn't break.

Not because they "got over it."
 Not because they forgave quickly.
 Not because they swept it under a spiritual rug labeled
"growth."

They didn't break
 because they let the rupture do its full damage.

They didn't skip steps.

They sat in the grief.
 Let the rage live in the room without trying to manage it.
 Held conversations that lasted all night
 and didn't fix anything by morning.

They stopped being polite.
 Stopped pretending everything was working.
 Stopped managing each other's perception.

And for the first time in their marriage —
 they started telling the truth.

Not just about the affair.
 About *everything*.

The pressure.
 The loneliness.
 The way they both stopped trying long before anything "went wrong."

And something happened in that raw, messy, sleepless terrain
 that never happened in all the years they got it "right":

They *met* each other.

Most people think relationships end when someone betrays the other.
 But that's not always true.

Sometimes betrayal isn't the end —
 it's the *mirror*.

It shows you what's been ignored.
 It exposes the ways you've already left each other quietly, long before the big break.

And if you're brave enough not to run,
 not to fix,
 not to disappear into blame or performative repair —

you might find something deeper underneath the wreckage:

Not the relationship you *had*.
The relationship that's finally *real*.

They didn't go back to what was.
They built something new.

A partnership where nothing was assumed.
Where tenderness wasn't an obligation, but a choice.
Where failure wasn't the end of love — it was the beginning of *truth*.

~~~~~

Some couples don't make it because they fail.
Others don't make it because they never learn how.

The ones who do —
are the ones who finally stop trying to be perfect,
and start learning how to stay honest when everything else falls apart.

~~~~~

The Myth of the Unbreakable Bond

You've been chasing the wrong metric.

You think a great relationship is one that doesn't break.
 One that stays steady, clear, and composed.
 Where trust is never lost.
 Where mistakes are minor.
 Where growth is linear.

That's the myth.

And like all myths built on perfection —
 it quietly destroys the very thing it's trying to protect.

Because real love doesn't happen inside unbrokenness.
 It happens *after the break*.

After the letdown.
 After the lie.
 After the silence that lasted too long.
 After the truth that was buried for years finally makes its way out.

The best relationships aren't the ones that avoided all damage.
 They're the ones that *learned how to repair*.

They don't wear their flawlessness like a badge.
 They wear their *resilience like a scar that healed stronger than the skin around it*.

High performers hate this.

Because it means no matter how perfect you are,
 you'll still fail your partner sometimes.

You'll say the wrong thing.
 You'll miss a need.
 You'll protect yourself instead of showing up.
 You'll project. Avoid. Collapse.
 You'll betray — not always with your body,
 but with your absence.

And when that happens,
 your success strategies won't save you.
 Your intelligence won't fix it.
 Your insight won't undo the rupture.

Only one thing will:

Your capacity to repair.

Repair doesn't mean restoring what was.
 It means *building what wasn't there before.*

It means facing the part of you that hurt them.
 Sitting in the discomfort of impact.
 Letting them grieve.
 Letting yourself grieve.

It means not rushing to resolution —
 but staying in the mess long enough for something new to emerge.

You don't build an "unbreakable" bond.
 You build a *trustworthy* one.

One that can be dropped, tested, stretched —
and still return stronger.

Because the goal of love isn't perfection.
It's *durability.*

And durability doesn't come from never failing.
It comes from knowing how to come back from it —
together.

~~~~~

*Strong relationships aren't the ones that never
break.*
*They're the ones where breaking becomes a
doorway —*
not an ending.

~~~~~

Esther Perel and the Architecture of Repair

Esther Perel doesn't romanticize betrayal.
She doesn't justify it.
But she does understand it.

She sees infidelity not only as a violation —
but as a revelation.

A turning point.
A rupture that doesn't just show you what broke —
but what was never truly whole.

And that's what makes her work so radical.

Because she doesn't just ask:
"How do we recover from this?"
She asks:
"What is this showing us about what we never built?"

Perel teaches that betrayal isn't always a collapse of love.
Sometimes, it's the collapse of an *illusion.*

Of perfection.
Of unspoken needs being magically met.
Of roles you never consented to but silently played.

And once the illusion dies,
you have two choices:

- Abandon the relationship because it no longer matches your fantasy.

- Or — build something real in its place.

Something that doesn't rely on performance.
Something that doesn't require perfection.
Something that can hold *all of you* — even the broken parts.

This is the architecture of repair:

It's not just apologizing.
It's not just going to therapy.
It's not just earning back trust.

It's **building a new foundation** —
with different truths, different terms, different levels of
emotional honesty.

You don't just restore the relationship.
You *renovate* it.

Tear down the false walls.
Open new rooms.
Let in more air.
More truth.
More contradiction.
More *you.*

Perel says:
*"Your first marriage is over. Would you like to create a
second one — with the same person?"*

That's not just about infidelity.
That's about *every rupture* we try to deny, smooth over, or
avoid.

Because every time we avoid the work of repair,
we're choosing the comfort of pretense
over the discomfort of truth.

And no matter how polished your life looks,
you cannot outsource *intimacy with reality.*

This is the invitation:

When something breaks —
don't rush to tape it up.

Ask:

- *What truth has this made unavoidable?*

- *What patterns have finally surfaced?*

- *What version of us needs to die — so something more honest can live?*

That's repair.
Not recovery.
Reconstruction.

~~~~~

Repair isn't the return to what was.
It's the commitment to build what should've been there all along.

~~~~~

What Real Repair Requires

Most people think repair is a conversation.

"I'm sorry."
"I understand what I did."
"I'll do better."
"Let's move forward."

But if you've ever tried to fix something too quickly,
you know that words can sound perfect
and still land hollow.

That's because **repair isn't language.
It's a process.**

A *slow*, *uncomfortable*, *honest* return
to connection —
not to what you had,
but to what you've never built before.

Here's what real repair actually requires:

1. Responsibility

Not just for what happened —
but for the *impact*.
You don't get to decide how much it hurt them.
You don't get to skip the parts that feel out of proportion.
You own the ripple, not just the rock.

> *"I didn't mean to" is explanation.
> *"I see what it did to you" is repair.*

2. Grief

Real repair involves mourning.
You don't just "move on."
You *let something die* —
a version of the relationship, of you, of the illusion that this
was flawless.

You cry. You rage.
You sit in the wreckage long enough to understand
what this moment actually cost both of you.

Without grief, forgiveness is performative.
And without grief, nothing grows.

3. Patience

Your partner won't come back on your timeline.
You don't earn trust back by demanding it.
You show up *without the guarantee that it will be received yet*.
You stay consistent.
You stay soft.
You stay available — not to fix their pain, but to *witness it*.

4. Transparency

No more managing perception.
No more half-truths.
No more "protecting them from the full story."
Repair doesn't require oversharing — but it *does* require honesty.

If they don't have the truth,
they don't have a choice.
And if they don't have a choice,
they can't fully return.

5. Co-creation

Repair isn't "getting back on track."
It's building something new — together.

You ask:

- *What do we want this to be now?*

- *What new agreements do we need?*

- *What do we both need to feel safe again — not just seen?*

That's how repair becomes *relational evolution*, not emotional avoidance.

You don't graduate from rupture.
You walk through it, hand in hand —
sometimes in silence,
sometimes in grief,
but always toward something more *real* than what came before.

~~~~~

Repair doesn't happen when you say the right thing.
It happens when you stay through the part where nothing feels right yet —
and choose to keep loving anyway.

~~~~~

Choosing Again

There is a quiet courage
in choosing someone twice.

Not because they never hurt you.
Not because it's easy.
Not because everything makes sense now.

But because something deeper has emerged
on the other side of rupture:

Truth.

The performance is gone.
The illusion has shattered.
And all that's left is two people
standing in the emotional rubble,
deciding if they're still willing
to *build.*

This is the moment most relationships never reach —
not because they failed,
but because they never went deep enough to confront the
choice beneath the story.

You didn't stay because of the history.
You didn't stay because it's easier than leaving.

You stayed because you *chose again.*

With new eyes.
With less fantasy.
With more honesty.
With the kind of maturity that says:

"I see who you really are now.
And if you're willing — I'd like to walk forward with you, not as we were…
but as we are."

Every great love has these moments.

Moments where it would've been easier to leave.
Where disappointment made staying look like foolishness.
Where staying required more humility than pride usually allows.

But the strongest relationships aren't built on always getting it right.
They're built on the willingness to *return.*

Not to the beginning.
But to the *choice to love each other now — in this version of the truth.*

That's what "choosing again" means.

It's not passive.
It's not convenient.
It's not even romantic most of the time.

It's spiritual.
It's gritty.
It's sacred.

And it's the foundation of any relationship
that hopes to last longer than its first illusion of perfection.

~~~~~

*The couples who make it
aren't the ones who never hurt each other.
They're the ones who learned how to say,
again and again:

"I still choose you."*

~~~~~

Building Intimacy Without Losing Yourself

The Disappearing Act

She didn't leave because he was cruel.
 Or absent.
 Or volatile.

She left because she couldn't feel herself anymore.

She used to be fire.
 Unapologetic. Sharp. Brilliant.
 She built companies. Raised money. Made hard calls with grace.
 Everyone trusted her to lead.

But at home, over time, she became… soft.
 Then careful.
 Then small.

He never asked her to change.
 But somehow, she did.

She deferred more. Smiled more.
 Asked fewer questions.
 Apologized before expressing a need.

And when she finally left, it wasn't with rage —
 it was with confusion.

Not about *him*.
 About *herself.*

"I don't know when I started disappearing," she told a friend.
"But I don't think I've been in the room for years."

This is the heartbreak most high performers don't know how to name:

Not losing the relationship.
 But losing yourself inside it.

And it rarely starts loud.

It starts with compromise.
 With being "understanding."
 With saying *"This isn't a battle worth fighting."*

It starts with believing that softness means silence.
 That surrender means stillness.
 That connection requires contraction.

You think you're being a "good partner."
 You think you're finally doing the emotional work.
 You think this is what maturity looks like.

But inside, something is eroding.

You stop saying what you really think.
 You stop being fully expressed.
 You start molding yourself to avoid conflict, disappointment, distance.

And the version of you that's alive out there —
  leading, building, creating, thriving —
  is nowhere to be found at home.

This is the disappearing act.

The quiet, unspoken decision
  to be loved *safely*
  instead of living *fully*.

It's what happens when the price of closeness becomes
too high —
  and the only way to stay connected
  is to slowly vanish.

And the truth is,
  if someone loves a version of you that isn't fully real,
  it will never feel like love anyway.
  Just approval.

And approval is a poor substitute for intimacy.

~~~~~

> *If you have to disappear to stay close,*
> *you're not in love —*
> *you're in emotional exile.*

~~~~~

Why High Performers Go Numb in Love

It doesn't happen all at once.

You don't wake up one day and think,
 "I'll stop sharing what I need."

You just stop sharing the *third time* it gets misunderstood.
 The fifth time it sparks tension.
 The tenth time it's met with silence.

So you adapt.

You become less reactive.
 More "understanding."
 You let things slide.
 You start calling it maturity.

But it's not maturity.
 It's numbness.

And numbness is what high performers choose
 when connection feels like a threat
 to their *sense of self.*

You've spent your whole life earning space by being sharp,
clear, competent, impressive.
 That identity *works.*

So when emotional closeness asks you to be something
else —
 raw, contradictory, needy, open —
 you hesitate.

Because who are you
 if you're not holding everything together?

Who are you
 when you don't know how to fix what you're feeling?

So instead of letting the emotion rise,
 you flatten it.

You downplay it.
 Label it irrational.
 Package it into something more manageable —
 or more "respectable."

You trade your instincts for insight.
 Your voice for neutrality.
 Your fire for "stability."

And in doing so, you lose something precious:

Your **aliveness** in the relationship.

This is why so many high performers go numb in love:

Because they've never learned how to be *fully expressed*
 without also being punished, misunderstood, or made to
feel *too much*.

So they do what they've always done when things feel
unsafe:

They over-function.
 They under-reveal.

They maintain the connection
by *modifying themselves out of it.*

But connection isn't safe because you shrink.
It's safe because you're allowed to stay *fully present*
without being penalized for it.

Your relationship isn't working if it only loves you
when you're easy to receive.

It's working when you can bring all of you —
complex, dynamic, messy —
and still be *welcomed.*

~~~~~

> *You didn't go numb because you stopped
> caring.
> You went numb because you believed you
> couldn't stay whole
> and still be loved.*

~~~~~

Glennon Doyle and the Unbecoming

Glennon Doyle had it all.

A bestselling memoir.
A family.
A platform built on truth-telling and redemption.
She was the poster child for overcoming struggle —
for finding wholeness through healing.

And then... she left.

Not because her life was falling apart.
 But because *she was disappearing inside it*.

She describes the experience not as a breakdown,
 but as an *unbecoming*.

Unbecoming the woman the world praised.
 Unbecoming the partner who kept the peace.
 Unbecoming the persona that made her lovable —
 but not *visible.*

And in that unbecoming,
 she found something terrifying and holy:

The truth.

She fell in love with someone unexpected.
 She disrupted the story people wanted from her.
 She chose freedom over optics.
 She chose *honesty* over harmony.

And in doing so, she showed the world — and her readers
 —

 what intimacy really requires:

Not sacrifice.
 Not perfection.
 Not the performance of closeness.

But *self-revelation.*

Glennon didn't leave because she didn't value love.
She left because she finally understood what love requires:
You.
Fully.
Unapologetically.
Even if that self shakes the structure.

She wrote:

> *"Perhaps women have to unlearn everything they've been taught about what it means to be good, in order to be free."*

And for high-performing women especially,
that message is atomic.

Because so many of them have earned safety, love, and recognition
through performance.

And intimacy — true, raw, nothing-held-back intimacy —
is the one place performance becomes prison.

You don't need to leave your relationship to unbecome.
But you do need to check:

- Have I stopped expressing my full self to keep the peace?

- Have I confused adaptability with love?

- Have I shaped myself so well to what they need, that I no longer know what I *want?*

Because if the only way to stay connected
is to become someone else,
you're not connected.
You're contained.

And love that contains you isn't love.
It's a holding cell.

~~~~~

Real love doesn't ask you to stay small.
It invites you to bring your whole self to the
table —
and trusts that truth won't destroy the
relationship.
It will finally make it real.

~~~~~

Boundaries as Bridges, Not Walls

High performers are used to control.
They don't ask for much.
They hold it together.
They protect the room from their needs.

So when things get hard,
they don't set boundaries —
they set expectations.
Or they build walls.

Walls of silence.
Walls of withdrawal.
Walls that look like "space," but feel like absence.

Because somewhere along the way,
 they learned that asking for what you need
 might cost you connection.

Or worse — make you look *weak*.

But here's the truth:
 A boundary isn't a wall between you and your partner.
 It's a bridge between your truth and their presence.

Boundaries aren't ultimatums.
 They're invitations.

They say:
 "Here's what keeps me grounded."
 "Here's what helps me feel safe."
 "Here's what I'm still healing — and how I need you to meet me there."

And in healthy love, that clarity doesn't push someone away.
 It gives them something solid to walk across.

The reason boundaries feel threatening in relationships
 is because we confuse them with control.
 With punishment.
 With distance.

But when offered honestly —
 boundaries *build trust.*

They let both people remain whole.
 They make sure no one disappears into the other.

They allow each of you to bring your full self forward,
without getting lost inside the connection.

You don't need to be available all the time.
 You don't need to say yes when your body says no.
 You don't need to share everything just to prove you're
open.

Boundaries are how you stay in the room —
 without abandoning yourself to stay there.

And the most intimate relationships aren't the ones with no
boundaries.
 They're the ones where the boundaries are known,
respected, and *spoken out loud.*

You don't need to shrink to be loved.
 You don't need to vanish to feel safe.
 You don't need to perform agreement to avoid conflict.

You need to be fully visible
 and deeply respected — at the *same time.*

That's what boundaries make possible.

~~~~~

> *A wall says "stay out."*
> *A boundary says "come closer — here's how*
> *to love me well."*

~~~~~

Staying Fully You, Fully In

You don't have to choose anymore.

You don't have to choose between being fully loved
 and fully expressed.
 Between being powerful
 and being vulnerable.
 Between being a whole person
 and being in a relationship.

That was the false choice.
 That was the performance you were taught to live inside.

But the truth?

**You can bring all of yourself —
 and stay.**

And when you do,
 your relationship doesn't get weaker.
 It gets *real.*

Because now, what's being loved isn't your performance.
 It's *you.*

This is what intimacy actually asks for:

Not that you melt into each other.
 Not that you merge.
 Not that you disappear in the name of closeness.

But that you stand side by side,
 fully revealed,
 and say:

*"I see you. I hear you. I'm still me.
And I'm still in."*

The highest form of love
is not self-sacrifice.
It's self-anchored connection.

Two people who haven't collapsed into each other —
but who choose, over and over again,
to show up without hiding.

That's where the fire lives.
That's where the trust grows.
That's where the real story begins.

You can still have your edge.
You can still have your ambition.
You can still have your boundaries.
And you can bring *all of that* to someone who is strong enough
not to be intimidated by your wholeness —
but *invited into it*.

Let this be the final shift:

You don't have to keep trying to earn love
by being easier to love.

You don't have to lose yourself to keep someone close.

You can stay fully you.
And fully in.

That's not the compromise.
That's the *miracle*.

~~~~~

*The relationships that last
aren't the ones where nobody changes —
but the ones where both people
become more of themselves
inside the love they're building together.*

~~~~~

Epilogue: The Quiet After

You made it to the end.

Not of your work.
 Not of your relationship.
 Not of the questions.

But the end of something else —
 the illusion that closeness can be controlled.

That love is earned through mastery.
 That if you just listen better, fix faster, lead smarter…
they'll stay.
 You'll feel safe.
 You'll feel *worthy.*

But now you know:

You were never supposed to optimize love.
 You were supposed to *feel* it.
 Risk it.
 Let it change you.

You don't need another strategy.

You don't need to highlight this book or quote it in conflict.
 You don't need to redesign your calendar, or create a new
set of rituals.

You just need to *show up softer.*
 Say what's true, even when it's messy.
 Stay a few seconds longer in the silence.
 Let the moment hurt a little before you fix it.

Let them reach for *you*, not your insight.

And when you miss it — because you will —
 come back without shame.

That's what the strongest people do.

Not control every moment.
 But *return* to it
 with more honesty than last time.

You don't need to become someone else.
 You need to bring more of *yourself*
 to the places you used to hide.

That's it.

The goal isn't to be perfect.
 The goal is to be **present enough**
 to build a relationship that can hold real life, not just your
best self.

There's no applause here.
 No checklist.

Just a quiet question, left ringing in the air:
 Now that you know, will you love differently?

~~~~~

You already know how to lead.
Now, let's see how brave you are

when there's nothing left to control —
only something left to feel.

~~~~~

Suggested Reading

The ideas in this book are in conversation with the work of many brilliant minds. For readers who want to go deeper, challenge their patterns, or explore love from different angles, here are a few essential companions:

On Love, Intimacy, and Repair

- *The State of Affairs* by Esther Perel

- *Mating in Captivity* by Esther Perel

- *Attached* by Amir Levine and Rachel Heller

- *Hold Me Tight* by Dr. Sue Johnson

- *The Seven Principles for Making Marriage Work* by Dr. John Gottman

On Selfhood and Emotional Honesty

- *Untamed* by Glennon Doyle

- *The Gifts of Imperfection* by Brené Brown

- *Radical Acceptance* by Tara Brach

- *Set Boundaries, Find Peace* by Nedra Glover Tawwab

On Leadership, Systems, and the Limits of Optimization

- *Principles: Life and Work* by Ray Dalio

- *The 4-Hour Workweek* by Tim Ferriss (especially as a cultural artifact)

- *Atomic Habits* by James Clear (for its systems approach — and what it can't fix)

Memoirs and Moments That Reveal the Private Behind the Public

- *Becoming* by Michelle Obama

- Interviews and tributes to Robin Williams

- Public statements and reflections by Dwayne "The Rock" Johnson

- Articles on the personal lives of high-profile leaders like Elon Musk, Anna Wintour, and Steve Jobs

About the Author

Ethan Starke is a strategist, storyteller, and emotional translator for high performers.

With a background that bridges entrepreneurship, coaching, and creative leadership, Ethan has spent over two decades helping ambitious people confront the very things their success was never built to handle — vulnerability, connection, and real intimacy.

He doesn't believe in fixing people.
He believes in telling the truth so clearly, it can't be ignored.

This is not his first book.
But it may be the first one that was written without a mask.

To learn more or connect with Ethan, visit:
ethanstarke.com